A NEW WITCH'S GUIDE TO CRAFTING THE FUTURE

A NEW WITCH'S GUIDE TO CRAFTING THE FUTURE

A NEW WITCH'S GUIDE TO CRAFTING THE FUTURE

A NEW WITCH'S GUIDE TO CRAFTING THE FUTURE

CHAWEON KOO
구자원

SPELL BOUND

Smith Street Books

OPENING RITE
6

WOOD
12

FIRE
56

EARTH
102

METAL
148

WATER
198

CLOSING RITE
246

OPENING RITE

I call upon my ancestors, who have created that which is me.

Let my words guide you, the reader,
    to reclaim your birthright: magic.

Witch: *mah nyuh* 마녀

This book is organized
To reflect the forces of entropy
Of a cosmos that is ever-changing.

Meet the 5 phases of Chinese wuxing:

1. *Wood* – a time of robust growth, like spring days
2. *Fire* – swelling with hot passion and energy, like the summer Sun
3. *Earth* – grounded enough to support the transition to late summer
4. *Metal* – organized, structured, ready to harvest in the autumn
5. *Water* – falling into the mystical stillness of winter

Each phase moves
               into the
                     next.

Meet the 3 phases of Western alchemy:

1. *Nigredo* – the burning, the darkening, the fermenting, the breaking down of a substance
2. *Albedo* – it suddenly turns to white ash, a flash of insight
3. *Rubedo* – now in a purified form, reinvigorated and reanimated

Don't rush through the phases.
The process cannot be sped up.

Mah nyuh 마녀

Magic is not a safe space.
Magic is more like a great pyre
A tidal wave
A meteorite hurtling
Through the atmosphere
At 30,000 mph.

Magic expects you to put in the effort.

Get used to the f o r m l e s_s
That suddenly crystallizes
And d i s i n t e g r a t e
Yet again
   And again
         And again.

Mah nyuh 마녀
Your body is built to work with your mind
So that you can focus on your True Will.

I snatched that phrase from Thelema,
A philosophy developed by occultist Aleister Crowley.
Crowley was not a woke person
But magic is about saving the slippery baby
While throwing out the grungy bathwater.

Mah nyuh 마녀

There is no safe space,
No fully affirmative place in magic.
It thrives in contradictory nuance.

Mah nyuh 마녀

Your True Will is unique,
A lifelong journey of self-acceptance.
Magic is the aphrodisiac
That makes you pant, with desire,
For every morsel of yourself.

(Even the parts that make you cringe)

Play with reality
Glide with curiosity,
From one experience to the next
Lipgloss poppin', of course.

Mah nyuh 마녀

Study the compass from SSOTBME by Ramsey Dukes.
It shows that magic thinking is different from:

Artistic thinking,
Scientific thinking,
Religious thinking,
But don't fret; they all lie on a spectrum.

This compass says:
Magic is about results you can observe.
What you can measure.

Magic makes things happen.

But you ask, is magic real?
As if there is just one criteria to judge everything.

As if the Mona Lisa should be judged
like the Higgs boson.

Instead, take your dagger
and cut a magic circle around you
that transcends
              time
                  and

   space.

In it, you dance,
As magic grabs your hips
To gyrate with you.

NIGREDO

DURING THE DAY, MANGURI
PARK LOOKS MUCH LIKE THE REST
OF NORTHERN SEOUL'S NATURE,
WITH LOW MOUNTAINS COVERED IN
DECIDUOUS TREES.

THERE ARE PUBLIC TRAILS FOR
HIKERS TO ESCAPE THE FLASHING
BILLBOARDS, HIGH-RISE BUILDINGS,
AND TRAFFIC OF MODERN SOUTH
KOREAN LIFE.

BUT I WAS

THERE AT

MIDNIGHT,

WHEN THE

TRAILS WERE

COMPLETELY

EMPTY.

신

I walked past a baseball field, fully lit, as if inviting spirits to play a game.

Manguri Mountain.

leading up

was a solitary path,

A few steps away

There were no lights. All I had was a dim flashlight and the Moon behind the clouds, her silver beams fading in and out.

Behind me, the safety of brightly lit skyscrapers and honking taxi cabs. In front of me, who knew what sort of axe murderers or blood-sucking animals waited in the shadows.

I had every reason to go home. Instead, my legs compelled me up the uneven steps, to the public cemetery on the mountain.

As I climbed, the brightness of the modern, rational world receded further and further behind me, as if I was no longer in 2017. As if I was back in the old days, when *dokkaebi* 도깨비 and jumping ghosts haunted the forests.

Wherever I turned my flashlight, I would catch the reflection of wild eyes, hear the sound of claws scattering as my own feet scrammed into a pathetic run. There was nowhere to go but up, deeper into the forest, to the trees in the distance that stood like burned skeletons. The night air was eerily silent, punctuated only by a sound like a cross between the spring wind and the snarl of a Lovecraftian creature.

I sat down on a bench, trying to calm my shaking hands as I lit candles. I was here to do a banishing spell, and I'd be damned if I came all this way to be scared off by the orbs of light, darting around the ink-black silhouette of the treeline.

Then suddenly, the Moon brightened, the clouds parted, and on my left as far as my eyes could see, were mounds.

For much of Korean history, they didn't dig graves. They piled dirt onto the bodies.

I   WAS   A   WITNESS   TO

A   FIELD   OF   KOREAN   ANCESTORS.

FOR THE NEW WITCH JUST BEGINNING THEIR JOURNEY, THE NATURAL PLACE TO START IS WITH THEIR ANCESTORS ✦

ANCESTORS

For the new witch just beginning their journey, the natural place to start is with their ancestors.

You are reading this with a body created by your ancestral DNA. The cranky old woman in the family albums, the one who died before you were born: she is essential to your magic because she created your flesh and blood.

A lot of people aren't able to fill out a family tree. I am one of those people. I am part of the Korean diaspora, the seven million ethnic Koreans who ended up scattered from the motherland, especially after the Korean War.

Many people are adopted, or come from families where sharing information is difficult. There might be exaggerations or straight up falsehoods in family records. Relatives may have been abusive. The process of detangling blood ancestry can be far more complicated than simply opening a book about an exotic tradition that we can escape into.

If that's the case for you, I suggest looking way back into your family tree. Ancestors don't have to be recent, and you don't have to know their names – look at who used to live in your ancestors' general region, instead.

When possible, even if it's just a passing clue about our home country, it's vital to our magic that we learn about our ancestors. The experiences of my grandmother passed into the DNA of my mother, which then passed on to me. I can't avoid being affected by my family's history, because my body is literally shaped by their genes and stories.

This isn't to say that blood ancestry is the only thing that matters. Italian-American witch Mallorie Vaudoise writes in *Honoring Your Ancestors* that we have multiple lineages, including the cultural and intellectual. Many British rock guitarists credit Black American blues musicians from the Mississippi Delta as their cultural ancestor. Some Western psychologists credit Buddhist texts as their intellectual predecessor.

These cultural ancestors should not be discounted. But starting with your blood ancestry builds a solid foundation that you can lean on in your magic.

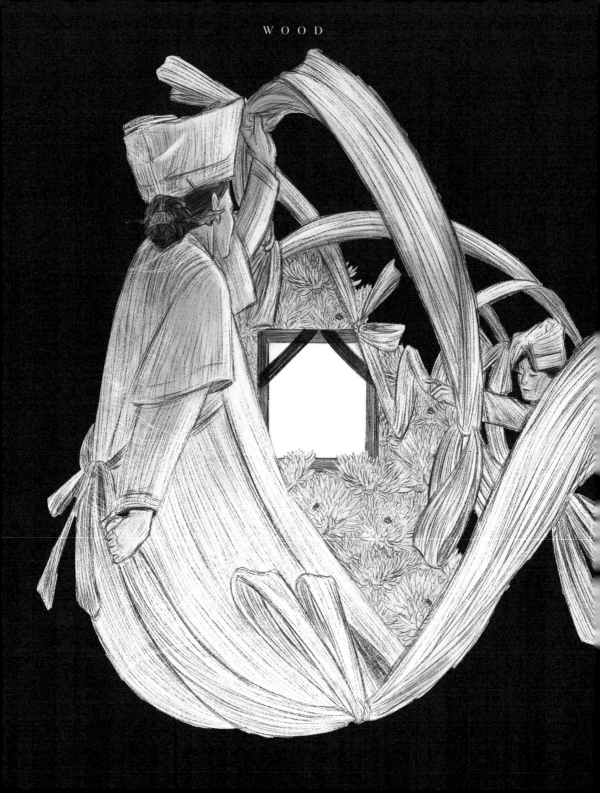

MOTHERLAND

Holy mountains stretch across the eastern coast of the Korean Peninsula, which were considered the spine of the country. But now, its back is broken by the DMZ: the world's most heavily fortified military border, which separates North and South Korea.

Our ancestral tree doesn't just include people. It's also the land where they lived, died, were colonized, starved, and survived. The flora and fauna of that land is made up of their ancestors before them, whose flesh and bones turned to dust and soil.

Looking at those graves on Manguri Mountain, I was overcome with a rage that I had never felt before: like a rumble in the Earth before it splits open and demons fly out from the open gash. It was an intense emotion, a hate–grief right below the surface, ready to explode with chthonic fury.

This was *han* 한. Stepping onto my ancestor's land, I could feel their anger and injustice and agony.

Han 한 is Korean in name, but it exists everywhere. Even if we haven't experienced abuse ourselves, we still feel it in our blood: the trauma our mother experienced, and her mother, and hers.

Maybe I had to breathe in the spores, the dust of my ancestors' bodies into my own, before I could claim to be a witch. After all, epigenetics has shown that much of our DNA stays dormant until triggered by the environment.

Of course, visiting overseas graveyards isn't always necessary. What's important is to dig down into your emotional inheritance, through your blood's legacy. That's where you'll find the roots of your magic.

BANISHING SPELL

I didn't go to Manguri Mountain to find my ancestors. The whole reason I was even there was to do a banishing spell.

Just a few months before, I had started a *mukbang* 먹방, a Korean word meaning 'eating room,' on YouTube. 'Witches & Wine' was supposed to be me and my friend, noshing and gabbing around Seoul. I had no idea that it would soon become an all-witch channel, but sometimes your ancestors find you.

Making videos was supposed to be fun, but it wasn't. I had never touched editing software before, so each video took two excruciating weeks to make. The biggest problem: I felt super uncomfortable in front of the camera, even with my friend next to me. I had a real fear of being seen.

The banishing spell was meant to help rid me of this. But looking at those graves on Manguri Mountain, I felt I had a deeper purpose. I made a promise to these dead bodies, who had suffered so I could be free. I promised them that I would be seen.

So, I did my spell and then walked away without looking back, into the white light of the baseball field that I had left in another life.

Without knowing where you come from, it's harder to figure out where you're going to go.

All my life, I wondered why I had felt this anger, simmering under the surface. But the banishing spell had sublimated that rage, alchemized it into magic. Walking back, I was now guided through the dark by this *han* 한: a gift from my ancestors.

Psychology and New Age spirituality often suggest that we get rid of these 'low vibes,' only positivity allowed! But I knew, deep in the marrow of my bones, that *han* 한 was a blessing for a witch. It was like electricity to power up my magic.

Chances are, if you're interested in witchcraft, that you have your own ancestral version of *han* 한 as well. To find it, you may have to dip into the past, but don't let that stop you. As fantasy novelist Sir Terry Pratchett wrote: a witch walks though a dark and dangerous forest, unafraid, because she is the most fearsome creature there.

She moves through life with impunity, with the support of ancestors who want her to thrive; they provide the fertile soil for the witch who starts as a seed, germinating underground.

9-DAY ANCESTRAL ELEVATION EXERCISE

Just because you die, it doesn't mean you stop evolving. In many traditions, the living are an important means to help the dead gain wisdom and make amends.

For Reverend Dr. Aaron Davis, a Christian minister who also practices African Traditional Religions and Solomonic and Greek Magical Papyri (PGM) sorcery, it was annual pilgrimages to the home and graveside of Harriet Tubman that nourished a growing awareness of his ancestors.

He says, 'connecting to [ancestors] hooks us in to a spiritual birthright everyone deserves.' This exercise may be especially helpful for those who have a complicated relationship with the recent dead. It's open to any ethnic background or spiritual tradition, and can be modified as you see fit.

Items

9 white tapers or 2 white glass vigil candles
1 stemmed wine glass

Instructions

1. Start on the floor. In any pleasing configuration, light the candles and fill the glass with water.
2. Recite nine prayers or songs. They can be rote like Hail Marys and Our Father, from your heart, or a combination. Let the candles burn down if tapers, or for at least an hour. Snuff them out if they are in a glass vigil. Only keep candles lit if you have a fire-proof set-up.
3. The next eight days, repeat step one and two, but before you start, raise the items a little higher each day. You can use shelves or stackable things like books to do this.
4. By day nine, the set up should be in one of the highest points in your home. Once that last candle is finished, then you can move the glass to a more permanent place like an ancestor table/shrine.

Note

* Do not use that glass for other purposes or other spirits.
* Only do one elevation at a time.
* If you get a sense that something else needs to be added to the ritual, that's probably your ancestors talking to you. Follow their requests.

ALBEDO

LIKE MOST WOMEN, I WAS TRAINED
TO REPRESS MY *HAN* 한.

AS CHINESE-AMERICAN AUTHOR AMY
TAN WROTE IN *THE JOY LUCK CLUB,*
'I WAS TAUGHT TO DESIRE NOTHING,
TO SWALLOW OTHER PEOPLE'S MISERY,
TO EAT MY OWN BITTERNESS.'

Ingesting that repression and shame came with a price. I had a litany of mysterious symptoms that board-certified doctors and psychiatrists couldn't diagnose properly.

Anger, when it's allowed to fester, is crude and imprecise. It's destructive. But when it's refined, it is a laser that cuts through even a lifetime of fear: of being seen as you truly are. Of potential.

Anger is intoxicating and powerful.

Han 한 is anathema to religion and most of modern spirituality, with all their well-meaning but shallow ideas, like the rule of threes. This is spiritual bypassing – using spirituality as an excuse to shame and repress what you consider as negative emotions.

> **" ANGER IS INTOXICATING AND POWERFUL "**

As a witch, you have no choice but to step into that anger, into that shame, into all those other emotions that might be tempting to run away from. This is a lifelong process of courage; I still run away sometimes. But the witch eventually turns back around and, with shaky knees, faces these emotions down.

As University of Texas professor Brené Brown said, courage is telling your story, authentically, from your heart. This is poetic when you consider that the word 'courage' comes from the French *coeur*: the heart.

A magic spell is a witch telling, or 'spelling out,' her True Will.

This spelling works best when we're clear about who we are, at our deepest levels. Because witchcraft, at its finest, is a technology to alchemize our emotions – especially the ones we try to bury.

SHADOW WORK

Refining this *han* 한 will determine whether your magic is constructive or destructive. This is where shadow work can be helpful.

Because 'shadow work' sounds eerie, many people use the term incorrectly. They talk about it as if you're just trying to accept your 'dark' or 'bad' side.

The term 'shadow' comes from Carl Jung, who used it to describe the unconscious mind: often the parts of ourselves dealing with sexual and bodily urges. Labeled as shameful and sinful, these are repressed from our conscious selves.

The shadow self and *han* 한 are deeply interrelated, manifesting in unhealthy patterns when they're not addressed; if, despite your best efforts, the past just repeats and your spellwork constantly backfires … that's the shadow self.

I first heard about shadow work, not through psychological resources, but through another witch: Dr. Carolyn Elliott, whose book *Existential Kink* contains shadow work techniques. Reading her book, I realized that the shadow is not the enemy. It's just in hiding, away from the light of our conscious awareness, which is why it can often feel like a nefarious puppet master pulling the strings of our lives without our consent.

To come into your True Will as a witch, you have to embrace all your sides: the good, the bad, the ugly. As you start to reclaim more and more of those hidden parts, you'll find that there's nothing 'wrong' with you. You simply weren't fully formed yet.

FEEDING YOUR DEMONS

My favorite way to do shadow work is via Feeding Your Demons™, a Tibetan Buddhist practice reworked for a contemporary Western audience by Buddhist teacher and American Lama Tsultrim Allione.

As the Lama recounts, Machig Labdrön, an 11th-century Tibetan woman, visited a monastery with a tree that not even the monks dared meditate under because of a fierce demon who lived in it. But one day, to everyone's horror, Machig suddenly had something like a giggling fit and decided to climb that tree. The demon was absolutely livid and gathered the hordes to attack Machig. But, instead of fighting, she simply offered her body as a sacrifice. Deeply impressed, the tree demon stopped the attack and they became good friends. Thus began the practice of *chöd*.

In the spirit of *chöd*, Feeding Your Demons™ is about showing compassion to the demons that torment you. These demons are the figurative shadows in your life that are draining you of energy, whether that's the demon of the dates who keep ghosting you, the pesky neighbor who blasts music at 3 am, or a constantly overdrawn bank account.

In 'How to Feed Your Demons,' an article for Buddhist site Lion's Roar, the Lama goes over the five steps:

01

Find the demon in your body: where in your body does your demon live? Give it a clear face and physical form.

02

Personify the demon: imagine the demon leaving your body, standing in front of you.

03

Become the demon: switch places with the demon. Step into its shoes, and then say (as the demon) what it is that you really want and need.

04

Feed the demon and meet the ally: go back into your body and turn it into nectar, to nourish the demon. Once it's fully satisfied, invite it to transform into a new form: a friend and ally. The ally should look and feel different from the initial demon. Now trade places again, and, from its perspective, say how it will help and protect you.

05

Rest in awareness: allow the ally to dissolve into light, which your body absorbs. Revel in this integration with your new ally.

WHEN LAMA TSULTRIM ALLIONE GUIDES THE AUDIENCE IN THIS MEDITATION, PEOPLE DON'T SIT STILL. THEY ARE ENCOURAGED TO PHYSICALLY CHANGE POSITIONS AS THEY CHANGE PERSPECTIVES.

Both the movement and the emotional willingness to offer yourself to your demons, almost like a lover, takes this technique out of the realm of abstract visualization, into change you can feel in your body. And at the end, you're able to see, with clarity, what those demons were all along: friends and allies in waiting.

A note: don't pick heavy memories of trauma, because these demons may be too intense to sit with on your own. This exercise should only be performed with moments you know you can hold alone.

SOUNDS OF CHAKRAS AND SUTRAS

Baby witches are often scared away from shadow work because it becomes too intense, too quickly. Sometimes, you're not ready to deal with specific demons, and may need to take the 'edge off' of your *han* 한 first.

SOUND CAN BE A GREAT WAY TO DO THIS.

When we process sound, it can be far more emotional and visceral than language. From a more magical perspective, Indian musician and yogi Russill Paul writes in *The Yoga of Sound* that 'sound is energy, and sound configures energy to give it form.' In spiritual traditions all around the world, spoken sound is sacred. In ancient Egypt, to speak was akin to casting a spell, because the breath is our very soul.

I started my own witchy shadow work via Baird Hersey's album *Waking the Cobra: Vocal Meditations on the Chakras*, which I would listen to while walking through the streets of Seoul. I would allow the sound of each track to travel into my body, and onto the corresponding chakra, while simultaneously visualizing the spinning centers and their meanings.

Soon after, I found a chakra tuner app by Jonathan Goldman, a pioneer in harmonics. This app plays vowels at certain frequencies. I spent hours intoning along, and delighted in how I could physically feel each chakra sonorously vibrating. I also found Solfeggio frequencies of chakras on YouTube, and I would hum these aloud (for example, the muladhara, or root chakra, is 396 Hz). I imagined these waves of sound, which I could literally feel inside the cavity of my body, loosening up and sweeping away any energy stuck inside my chakras.

After a few months, I tried another type of sound meditation: the Uṣṇīṣa Vijaya Dhāraṇī sūtra. Originating in India, it became widespread in China and the rest of East Asia. The dhāraṇī was developed out of deep compassion for all creatures, to heal our 'karmic debt.' It is said that all beings in the vicinity of this chant – every mammal, insect, and bacteria – will no longer have to suffer in their next incarnations.

" WHEN WE PROCESS SOUND, IT CAN BE FAR MORE EMOTIONAL AND VISCERAL THAN LANGUAGE "

KARMA ISN'T WHAT YOU THINK

✦

Modern spirituality claims that we must hold back negative emotions, because you don't want to 'build' karmic debt. But a witch doesn't worry that 'karma is gonna get you,' because that's not what karma even means.

The literal translation of karma is 'action,' and it's an ancient Indian word that means ritual and sacrificial action. Simply put, karma is the effect of all your actions (both good and bad): even the most minuscule, unintentional ones.

Karma is usually used as a synonym to mean 'sudden good/bad luck' or 'fate,' which is very much focused on this present life. However, the word was originally tied to Eastern religions, like Hinduism and Buddhism, which believe in reincarnation, and past and future lives affecting each other in non-linear and complicated ways. According to these religions, not all karma from this lifetime will manifest in the same lifetime.

Therefore, magic doesn't have a simple 1:1 cause and effect. Casting a hex doesn't automatically lead to negative consequences. Healing work doesn't always lead to rewards, either.

For about ten days at sunrise, I recited the dhāraṇī. Out of
curiosity, I added my own twist by chanting in conjunction
with modern techniques like TAT (Tapas Acupressure
Technique) and EMDR (Eye Movement Desensitization and
Reprocessing); it was a powerful combination. After a few
days, I felt like a germinated sprout that had finally broken
through the soil.

Utilizing sound in shadow work may seem too light, too easy;
a lot of us are used to a deeply analytical, intense process to
work through our shadow selves. However, I find that a lot
of shadow integration can be unnecessarily heavy, and that a
more playful technique disperses the dread. The key is to find
a tool that allows you not just to feel the *han* 한, but to let it
reform. It doesn't just need to stay in arrested development.

And remember, as you begin to dive in and explore the tools that
work for you: the point of shadow work is integration. You're
not trying to fix yourself. There is nothing to fix, because
the whole point of being alive is to have imperfections.
Otherwise, why not remain a perfect,

unblemished spirit,

floating

above

e v e r · y   t   h   i   n   g?

If you're going to practice magic that's super shiny and spiritually bypassed, where is the fuel? Magic is a seed, and the life inside needs a witch's True Will to break out of its shell, through the half-frozen soil. To signify that spring is here, that life is about to begin.

A warning: be very mindful of how you live with the anger of intergenerational trauma and the other parts of your shadow self. It can and will destroy people if they wallow in that acid of constant rage or shame. But a witch dips into their well of *han* 한 and those other emotions with purpose. To void it robs the witch of her inheritance.

A witch French-kisses both worlds – that of a sinner and saint. We live in the liminal space, the moist, fertile conjunction of dark and light. And in that embrace, wondering whether you are 'good' or 'bad' ceases to be interesting.

RUBEDO

MAGIC TRADITION ISN'T JUST A
LITANY OF INSTRUCTIONS. IT'S ABOUT
KNOWING THE ROOTS OF A SYSTEM:
UNDERSTANDING HOW TO WATER IT,
TO KEEP IT GROWING AND THRIVING.

TOO MANY YOUNG WITCHES
WANT TO START MAGIC WITHOUT
KNOWING EVEN ITS BASIC HISTORY,
LET ALONE THEIR ANCESTORS. SUCH
ROOTLESS PRACTICE IS LIKE STICKING
A CUT-OFF BRANCH IN THE GROUND
AND PRETENDING IT CAN BEAR FRUIT.

Magical *noonchi* 눈치 [눈치] requires a strong grounding in tradition — after all, it's hard to adjust gracefully on shaky feet. You can't live in the edenic past, but you also mustn't abandon it. A witch needs to adjust to you. These witches interact with magic as an inert relic of the past, not the real living tradition that's still transforming around us. To me, neither end of the spectrum is interesting. A witch needs to be contextually intelligent. In Korean, this is called *noonchi* 눈치, where you can take the temperature of a situation and adjust yourself accordingly, instead of forcing everyone to adjust to you.

On the other extreme, some young witches fetishize traditions, denying any innovations in magic. These are purity-culture witches. They do magic that is closer to LARPing than to the actual renegades who practiced thousands of years ago.

TEACHERS

One of the best ways to ground yourself in tradition is to find solid teachers.

I lived in Bali for about five months, and it is one of the most magical places I've been to. While there, I had the pleasure of getting to know a local Balinese woodworker named Nano.

He told me how, in his culture, many men decide to devote their lives to spiritual study after the age of 40. To do this, it's of the utmost importance to find a good teacher; books aren't enough. As Nano put it, without a teacher 'you will end up like one of those crazy men who are yelling and kicking at the trees.'

In Bali, I saw many of these crazy people, but they weren't the locals. They were the Caucasian North Americans and Australians who came to Bali for spiritual reasons, but who had no teacher. They flitted around, ungrounded beyond their copy of *Eat, Pray, Love*. Unlike the locals, who walked with gravitas and *noonchi* 눈치, these Westerners would step into Hindu rituals in bikinis and angrily complain after Bikram yoga class that tourists who pointed out the locals' poverty were 'messing up the high vibes.'

I've personally found several teachers, initially by reading their books and listening to in-depth podcast interviews. Later, I had the privilege of talking to some of them on my YouTube channel, and then taking their courses. While I find #witchtok and #witchesofinstagram entertaining, I don't use them as my primary source of information. Magic is one of those topics that requires more than a 60-second video to adequately explain.

But caveat emptor: the magic world is filled with con artists and wanna-be cult leaders. And unfortunately, many people go deep into magic when they are in a vulnerable place in their life. Often, there are mental health issues at play — people enter magic under a cloud of fantasy and illusions of grandeur. There might be psychiatric concerns, like undiagnosed schizophrenia.

This is an age of misinformation, and the amount of conspiracy theories in the spiritual community is mind-boggling. You owe it to yourself not to blindly trust — be discerning.

SOME RED FLAGS IN A MAGIC TEACHER

01

They take themselves too seriously. Nothing is a bigger red flag, because it shows an over-identification with self.

02

They claim to have experienced ego death. This is great for certain spiritual practices, but magic is about aligning reality to your True Will, and to do this, we need that ego — just not too much of it.

03

They only go with their intuition, and avoid reading about/ studying magic. Reading and learning about other people's well-researched opinions does not stifle your own intuition — in fact, it gives it more room to grow because it provides a safe structure. Good teachers are a great balance of both objective study and subjective experience.

04

They only teach 'high vibes.' This is the junk food of magic. Witchcraft is not always pleasant.

05

Their personal life is a mess. Teachers don't have to be perfect; in fact, highly imperfect people often make the best teachers. However, if they aren't evolving in life, or are constantly embroiled in drama, then they don't have the bandwidth to be a clear vessel.

ROOTS

There's a lot of controversy about open vs. closed practices. Voodoo and other African Traditional religions (ATRs), certain shamanic traditions, and even tarot have been caught in the cross-hairs. Who is 'allowed' to practice these traditions?

This is like asking who's allowed to perform a Catholic exorcism. The priest is part of a closed practice. They are ordained, given secret initiations, and can do rituals that the layperson cannot. When people need an exorcism, they are not calling Fred from next door: they need an experienced priest from the diocese.

That doesn't mean you can't visit when the doors are open — anyone can participate in church ceremonies. But only the priest is empowered to lead the rituals.

Korean *mudang* 무당 go through a multi-day initiation, and then spend their lives devoted to the daily, hours-long task of working with gods and ancestors. A *mudang* 무당 from this background is very different from some random person who thinks it's cool and edgy to 'do what the shamans do.'

Cross-culturally, many initiates in closed traditions have experienced some sort of spirit sickness, suicidal thoughts, or even near-death experiences. It is not an easy road, and most of the initiates I've spoken to will admit that this is not a life they would wish on anyone else.

Part of that spirit sickness often comes from inter-generational trauma, especially when it hasn't had proper expression and closure. This is why ethnic heritage and blood ancestors are important. Without understanding the cultural and biological ancestral foundation of a tradition, its true meaning may simply be out of reach. Carl Jung wrote about how Westerners could not possibly understand the esoteric Indian mindset due to generations of Christianity; true or not, it's worth considering.

BECOMING AN INITIATED KOREAN MUDANG 무당

According to Mudang Jennifer Kim, one of the few initiated Korean shamans on TikTok, *mudang* 무당 have often gone through years of *shinbyung* 신병, which means 'spirit sickness,' suffering from mental and physical symptoms. Modern medicine and psychology don't seem to help, and it's only after they accept giving their life over to being a *mudang* 무당 that their *shinbyung* 신병 is brought under control.

'*Mudang* 무당 have the ability to channel the energy of the gods, i.e, conduct huge energy that would normally make a normal person insane or blow their fuse. Having an initiation is 'upgrading' a person's system, like putting in a surge protector to avoid blowing out the electricity,' Jennifer says.

Like all initiated practices around the world, it is impossible to decide for yourself if you should enter into it. You have to go to a *mudang* 무당, who will read your *jeum* 점 (your fortune). If you are called to be a *mudang* 무당, you will need to go through a very expensive (over $10,000), multi-day initiation ceremony.

These days, due to the growing popularity of *mudang* 무당, there have been advertisements for cheap(er) one-day initiations; they should be avoided if you want a traditional one.

But initiation is just the first step; the rest of your life, you will be learning from your godparent (your assigned teacher, often the person who initiates you). Finding the right godparent can be a long process and must not be rushed.

When non-initiates enter closed practices, they may get in over their heads and become one of those tree kickers. I've seen people lose jobs, lose relationships, and destroy their lives due to ungrounded spirituality. Always proceed with caution.

If you do want to learn more about closed practices, come with respect. You need to decide: will you be a Vanilla Ice or an Eminem? Both were white American rappers who had #1 hits, but one is widely ridiculed while the other is respected by the Black rap community as a legend. Don't dive in because you want clout: drop the entitlement and expectation that you should be accepted immediately. Instead, demonstrate the willingness to put in the hard hours.

If you find magical practices you think are interesting, enter those spaces ready to learn from the people who are already there, and know that some information may never be shared beyond initiated members.

That doesn't mean you can't be a student. It just means that your role there is to learn, not to control.

FUTURE BRANCHES

Magical *noonchi* 눈치 is often difficult for Westerners to accomplish, because their cultures espouse individualism. To avoid this trap, many well-intentioned young witches think they should try out every magic tradition, in an attempt to be open minded. However, this practice creates shallow magic. Instead, start with the solid foundation of your ancestral magic and see what other traditions call to you afterward. And then, perhaps most importantly, see how they all fit together in this modern world.

After all, magic doesn't stay old and static. It changes with the times. Magic cannot be controlled; it grows, wild, like forests of bamboo.

And that forest is changing quickly. What will happen to our ancestral DNA if the predictions of futurists like Ray Kurzweil manifest, and human consciousness can be transferred to robot bodies by 2045?

Can the past and the future survive, let alone thrive together? What happens to our ancestors' traditions in a world of silicon?

I found a shimmering thread of hope in Samseong-dong, a district of Seoul. South Korea is the world's most technologically advanced country, the home of companies like Samsung and LG, where 97 percent of the population is connected to high-speed internet.

On
the
grounds
of a millennia-old
Buddhist temple called
Bongeunsa, where you can
hear the bells chime and monks chant
throughout the day, there is a 75 foot Mireukbul
미륵대불, a statue of the future reincarnation of
Buddha. It was erected in 1986, to look over the skyscrapers
and COEX – a huge convention center that's also the largest
underground mall in the world, and once home to a museum
featuring hologram performances of Kpop stars. Tradition
and modernity exist so comfortably with each other in Seoul.
Legendary samurai Miyamoto Musashi says in *The Book of Five
Rings* that he doesn't follow one school. In the same vein, a
witch doesn't have to just follow one way – we can adjust
ourselves via *noonch*i 눈치, dipping into tradition while we
fly out into the here and now. Into the excitement of what
may be.
A witch first figures out the type of seed they are through
their ancestors.
Then they nurture that seedling by reaching
deep inside their *han* 한, integrating
that shadow to know themselves:
'*gnōthi sauton.*'

And then they break through: a tree, growing, growing, and reaching for the stars.

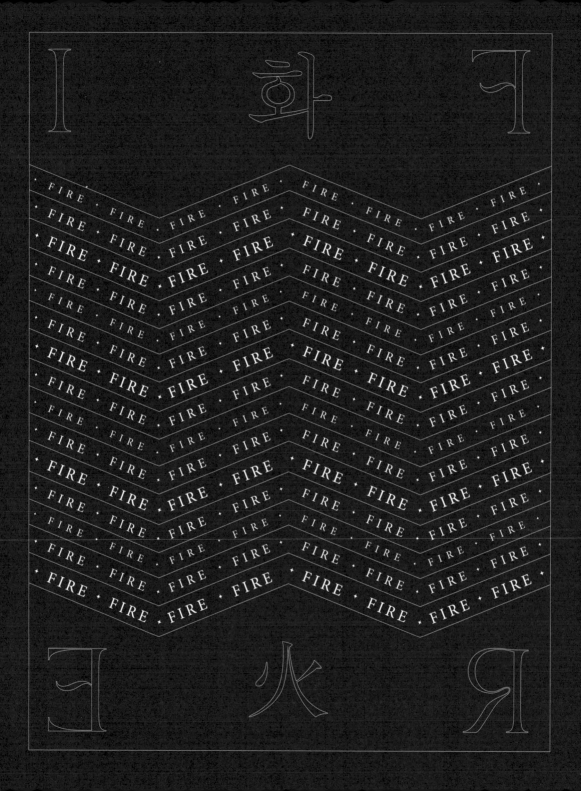

F 화 I

FIRE · FIRE · FIRE   FIRE · FIRE · FIRE
FIRE · FIRE · FIRE   FIRE · FIRE · FIRE
FIRE · FIRE · FIRE   FIRE · FIRE · FIRE
FIRE · FIRE · FIRE   FIRE · FIRE · FIRE
FIRE · FIRE · FIRE   FIRE · FIRE · FIRE
FIRE · FIRE · FIRE   FIRE · FIRE · FIRE
FIRE · FIRE · FIRE   FIRE · FIRE · FIRE
FIRE · FIRE · FIRE   FIRE · FIRE · FIRE
FIRE · FIRE · FIRE   FIRE · FIRE · FIRE
FIRE · FIRE · FIRE   FIRE · FIRE · FIRE
FIRE · FIRE · FIRE   FIRE · FIRE · FIRE
FIRE · FIRE · FIRE   FIRE · FIRE · FIRE

R E

NIGREDO

37,000 YEARS AGO, A GROUP OF
HOMO SAPIENS VENTURED INTO A
CAVE IN WHAT IS NOW THE ARDÈCHE
REGION OF FRANCE.

IN THE MOIST, PITCH-BLACK TUNNELS,
THERE WERE NECK-BREAKING
HOLES HIDDEN, AND FLASH FLOODS
THAT COULD DROWN EVERYONE
IN MINUTES.

AND YET THESE INTREPID HUMANS
INSISTED ON GOING EVEN DEEPER
INTO THIS WOMB OF MOTHER EARTH.

IN THE SHADOWY

HEART OF

CHAUVET CAVE,

THEY USED

CHARCOAL TO

DRAW FRESCOES

OF HORSES, DEER,

AND BISON.

마법

The pictures are stunningly realistic; the wall's natural texture was incorporated to recreate the rippling muscles of lions and mammoths, bears, and woolly rhinoceroses. Archaeologist and filmmaker Marc Azéma describes these paleolithic artisans as 'the very first naturalists' for documenting the flora and fauna of their world.

But Azéma also notes that, if you hold a flickering light to the walls, animals who had been drawn with additional heads and legs and tails animate. The reindeer gallop through the grasslands.

This may have been the *Homo sapiens*' first attempt at creating a movie; perhaps Chauvet Cave was a primitive Netflix. But deep inside, archaeologists found a bear skull, ritualistically placed atop a large stone. This was a sacred place.

As a witch, I can easily imagine this cave as the quintessential magical circle, where hunting parties would go when they needed to bring out the big guns for extra blessings, extra luck, and extra hype, when starvation was close and stakes were high.

For me, Chauvet Cave is where our ancestors worked with powerful rituals.

HIGH-STAKES MAGIC

Magic rituals have been called many things:

+ spells
+ petitions
+ law of attraction
+ prayers
+ fake-it-till-you-make-it
+ your 'process'

Thanks to Hollywood, rituals usually conjure up images of wild women under a Full Moon, dancing naked around a bonfire while chanting the names of pagan deities.

But rituals can also be small and subdued, like soft splashes from the kettle when you pour your meditation tea. Don't discount these everyday rituals; not long ago, the insta-fire of a stovetop would have been considered sorcery.

Rituals are all around us: the repeated and sequential actions we take, performed with sincerity and intent. Ritual is a building block of the parts of life that feel extra-alive, extra-special. It is the signal that something is important and deserves attention.

Yet, it also seems disingenuous to claim that preparing tea, no matter how pretty the cup or organic the leaves, is in the same category as smearing your menstrual blood over the front door in a trance.

I love smaller rituals: they are an integral part of witchcraft. However, I also encourage baby witches to try out the big, 'scary' ones as well. The beginning of your magical journey is a self-discovery process, and magic isn't cute and cuddly. Self-care may include magic, but not all magic is self-care.

As a beginner, you're trying to answer two questions:

1. What sort of ritual do I feel drawn to?
2. Does that ritual give me observable results?

Observable results are the whole point of magic. The ritual either gives you results or it doesn't; it's either high or low-performing. Otherwise, you're practicing some sort of religion, which is based on faith.

If you're going to be spending time on ritual, go for the high-performing. For some people, offering a daily stick of incense to local land spirits gives them great results. For you, this may be enough. But a lot of witches, through experimentation, learn they need something ... more. For me, incense does nothing, but I only learned this after a month of trying it out.

But whatever level of ritual they're at, witches can learn a lot from those like Dr. Rahul Jandial, a world-class brain surgeon.

In a podcast interview with Dr. Rangan Chatterjee, Dr. Jandial talks about his ritual the night before he goes into the operating theater.

He does postural exercises, because he will be hunched over for hours and wants to be physically ready. A lot of traditional magic, like performing surgery, is hard on the body; Korean shamans walk on knives and Western occultists spend hours conjuring spirits.

Dr. Jandial visualizes the surgery, and in the last ten minutes before falling asleep, he thinks about the 'shape' of the cancer he's going to cut out, and then lets his dreams prepare him for the inevitable unexpected.

When he gets into the operating theater, he doesn't just rely on technique. He also allows intuition to come through – he is bringing his A-game to the ritual of surgery.

Not all magical rituals require hours of this level of focus. But if you're too indifferent to results, or always play it safe even when you're not getting what you want, then you're missing out on the whole point.

> " KOREAN SHAMANS WALK ON KNIVES AND WESTERN OCCULTISTS SPEND HOURS CONJURING SPIRITS "

BASIC STRUCTURE OF RITUAL

Effective ritual starts with three components:

OPERATOR(S)

The person(s) doing the ritual. No matter how many operators, there is usually a leader, similar to the conductor of an orchestra. A skilled operator knows how to direct the energy created by the action of the ritual. Better yet, the operator is so in touch with their True Will — their deepest self's alignment with the collective Universe — that there is no need to direct anything. An uncomfortable truth: some people are naturals. Magic does not hand out participation trophies.

MEDIUM

Where the magic is happening, often called the magic circle. This space can be physical (the Chauvet Cave, the Hekate altar in your bedroom) or non-physical (the astral plane of dreams, an invisible magical circle that you draw with your hand). Ideally it's both. The non-physical space is essential, as you are literally cutting a new dimension in the fabric of reality: one that transcends space, time, and the laws of physics. This space is the incubator of the operator's True Will.

MESSAGE

The operator enters into the magic circle with a message. This message is portrayed through action, with words chanted, movement of the body, and tools like wands, plants, and animals to augment the experience. Some actions are spontaneous, but many have a well-established order.

Many baby witches focus too much on the embellishments in the message — the pretty crystals that they bought with money they should have used on their electricity bill or the chant they recite exactly as they found it on TikTok, even though it doesn't really excite them.

All three parts of the ritual are equally important, and they work together in magical synergy. Overemphasize one aspect to your detriment.

GUIDELINES ON HOW TO CRAFT A GOOD MESSAGE FOR YOUR RITUAL

Occultist and legendary comic book writer Alan Moore said that a spell is literally spelling a new reality.

Magic is observable, so you need it to be specific enough to measure. But if the message is too specific, it may stifle the magic. The message needs to be balanced.

Not good: I want to get a boyfriend (measurable, but too broad because you may get a man who lives on another continent, which is not what you want).

Not good: I want Jimin from BTS as my boyfriend (too specific).

Better: I want a boyfriend who looks like he could be a Kpop idol, who lives within driving distance from me.

Some people get caught up in past tense/present tense of the spell. I find that it doesn't really matter. The focus and intention is what's most important.

ANALYZING RITUALS

In magic, there are traditionalists who want to reconstruct rituals as closely as possible to the originals, barring modernity from entering. And then there are modernists who mainly follow their personal gnosis, because traditional spells are supposedly too old-fashioned and thus unnecessary.

The middle ground: remember that traditional rituals are products of their time. They carry important lessons and elements, but should also be allowed to evolve to suit their context.

In Korea, there is a ritual called *dol* 돌, which celebrates a baby's first birthday. It's a ritualistic representation of the baby's life as an adult: an array of items, including money, a book, glasses, and other objects representing professions, are laid out on the ground. In front of the extended family, the baby is encouraged to crawl and pick an item.

My young nephew had his *dol* 돌, and because we're Korean-American, the ritual was done differently than it is in South Korea. And those in South Korea do *dol* 돌 differently than families before the Korean War. But despite the differences, all of us are doing it fine; the point is to ask the Universe and ancestors to bless this fragile child, to allow them to have a long life.

This transformation of magic and ritual is everywhere you look: less than a generation ago, if your daughter became a *mudang* 무당, a Korean shaman, it was a huge family scandal. But these days, if a kid's mom is a *mudang* 무당, they're more likely to brag to their schoolmates about it.

And while Kpop idols don't practice their vocals by waterfalls like the *sorikkun* 소리꾼, who are the singers of *pansori* 판소리 (traditional Korean storytelling/theater), you can hear the influences of the drumming and emotive vocals in Kpop songs like Stray Kids' 'Thunderous,' (whose Korean title is literally *sorikkun* 소리꾼).

If we practice magical *noonchi* 눈치, the rituals that guide our magic stay dynamic, with the power to take on new meaning and abilities over time.

MAGIC

IS A

LIVING

TRADITION

THAT

NEEDS

TO BE

FANNED.

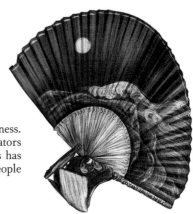

Today, we often do rituals without thought and self-awareness. These feel like a slog, and some modern commentators think that the lack of powerful, purposeful daily rituals has contributed to the shiftless, empty feeling that many people experience today.

Our ancestors would probably think us crazy for separating things like religion and government, education and magic, science and art. But as a witch, we don't see boundaries between 'magic rituals' and 'everyday life.' In my experience, they are one and the same: everyday life is a series of smaller magic rituals inside the larger magic ritual of living.

Consider how it's both wondrous and terrifying that you, the reader, are a sentient being who quivers and circulates energy, both inside your own body and into your environment. When you get up from your chair, the cushion will be warm where you touched it. Even at rest, you body is electric with the relentless, mysterious ritual of life ... and eventually the even more mysterious transformation of death

Don't ignore what's right in front of and inside of you: the basic human cell is the ultimate magical circle that we've carried from the Chauvet Cave. Successful rituals take time to build up to, but don't let that discourage you. Whenever you're in doubt, remember the whirring hum of your cells. Our bodies are where magic and ritual start: the ultimate altar to align reality to our Will.

ALBEDO

I WAS IN KINDERGARTEN WHEN
I FIRST SAW BOY GEORGE ON MTV.

HIS HAIR WAS FESTOONED WITH
COLORFUL RIBBONS, HIS FACE
PAINTED RED, GOLD, AND GREEN –
I HAD NEVER SEEN ANYONE LOVELIER.

NOT LONG AFTER, I UPGRADED
MY MALIBU BARBIE WITH AN
ASYMMETRICAL MOHAWK.

By the 1990s, pre-'Drag Race' RuPaul instructed me that I betta WERK in her songs. My weekly ritual consisted of watching daytime talk shows that featured Club Kids, a group of glittered fashion provocateurs who danced in a deconsecrated church re-named The Limelight. Within a few short years, drag culture and Club Kids were mainstream, aped by designers like Jean Paul Gaultier on high fashion runways. I shamelessly copied them all. With a full face of makeup, I was no longer just a plain, high school student in suburban Maryland. I was a high priestess, deep in ritual, as I painted blue glitter on my eyelids. I didn't talk the same, walk the same down school hallways, or even think the same. At the time, I didn't realize that I was in the throes of glamour magic.

GLAMOUR

Glamour magic is about rituals that utilize items like clothes, cosmetics, social media filters, photos, and videos. You, the operator, are creating sensual rituals to feel connected to your physical form. As dirt sorcerer Aidan Wachter writes in *Six Ways*, altars that look magical make you feel magical and therefore ARE magical.

One of the biggest differences I've found between the occult and the New Age is that modernity seems to strip the ritual. The old witches reveled in all its glittering baubles.

However, let's not get it twisted; the point of glamour magic is not the lipgloss or the twerking. Instead, it's to create a ritual that gets you in that magic circle and creates the mindset that makes magic the most effective.

Glamour magic doesn't just have to be visual, however. It encompasses all five of the senses, and is especially effective when they are used in conjunction; I have done rituals where I would look in the mirror and put on creams that smelled of flowers and felt like whipped cream on my skin. Textures, smells, tastes, and sounds will affect each person differently — the key is to find what heightens your own senses.

But regardless of the color of the glitter or the smell of the lotion, glamour magic is most effective when it is viewed as technology.

Technology isn't just about robots, or some dystopian sci-fi future. Technology is anything that extends the human mind and body in order to amplify human capacity. Some of our greatest technology is so simple and mundane, we may even discount it: the technology of fire cooks our food. The wheel extends our foot. Clothing protects our naked skin.

There's no need to build a cult around magic or being a witch.

MAGIC

RITUALS

ARE TOOLS

THE WAY A

HAMMER IS

A TOOL.

So instead of building an entire identity around being a witch, focus on getting really skilled with that hammer and find accessible ways, like beauty and glamour, to tap into magic.

There are those who are only concerned with the spirit – who reject glamour – but your body is your direct interface to the world. And your skin is just the top layer.

Occult publisher Scarlet Imprint's Alkistis Dimech has written about our occult body, which goes deeper than our flesh and holds the hidden mysteries of secret realms.

Glamour magic makes this occult body visible. It's the technology you can use to literally express your hidden self on your skin/sleeve: to bring the occult body up from the depths using clothes and makeup and movement as tools.

Wizards of the past were dressed in elaborate robes, not sweatpants. Even the act of meditating on a cushion, which seems low-key enough, is actually quite theatrical; the silence and the lotus position of your body signals that something out-of-the-ordinary is happening.

For new witches, over-the-top theatrics in glamour magic can be extremely helpful. A good rule of thumb for any sort of ritual: when you show up clean and groomed, the spellwork often ends up more successful. You wouldn't show up to a job interview like a slob and slouch in the chair, because it's important to you. Bring this mentality to magic.

KPOP

Now imagine a ritual in which magic circles are public, over-the-top spectacles. In the circle, beautiful creatures called 'idols' move in unison with intricate dances, transcending language barriers, slick studio production, and passionate live performance broadcasts that are uploaded on the collective conscious called the Internet. Right now, there is no magic more unadulterated than Kpop on such a massive scale. Their voices rise, casting spells – the lyrics are easy to remember, succinct, poetic and evocative. They are literally spelling out all the reasons you must love them, worship them. And all this is done with pyrotechnics, slick studio production, and passionate live performance broadcasts that are uploaded on the collective conscious called the Internet.

Kpop has helped make South Korea – a nation that had the GDP of Sudan back in the 1950s – one of the top cultural and economic powers of the world, all within my lifetime. If you have any doubt that glamour magic is powerful, just look at how it transformed an entire country.

Antonin Artaud wrote in *The Theater and Its Double* of how St. Augustine complained that the 'theater which, without killing, provokes the most mysterious alterations in the mind of not only an individual but an entire populace.'

Of course, St. Augustine may not have considered that Catholic mass is theater, as well. And then there's 2 Samuel 6:14 in the Bible – 'Wearing a linen ephod, David was dancing before the Lord with all his might.'

King David danced for God, the way Kpop stars dance for their fans. Preachers sermonize to their congregation as Kpop sermonizes to their YouTube audience. Kpop is both familiar and alien, overlaying Korean aesthetics on top of American pop.

But above all, it is EXTRA. It is about excess. It is as witchy as smearing blood on the doorway, though Kpop's occult body is strategically overlaid with glamour magic taken to the nth degree.

Back in the day, the Witches' Sabbath started as villagers dancing after a harvest or feast. The drawing of the magic circle, often done by ceremonial occultists, also used to be a dance. But somewhere along the way, with the formalization of magic (especially Western magic), hip gyrations were downsized.

But not in Kpop. They refined the body so that everyone from toddlers to hormone-overloaded teens to grannies could watch and fall in love.

Building on the work of drag queens and the Club Kids, Kpop idols have helped to redefine beauty and glamour for an entire generation. Back in the 1990s, the first wave of Kpop idols were forbidden to dye their hair and makeup was taboo.

But now, Kpop boy bands like SF9 are doing lipstick and foundation ads for MAC Cosmetics. These young men are held up as *kkonminam* 꽃미남, which literally translates to 'flower boys' – men admired for their alluring mix of masculine and feminine style.

"

IT IS AS WITCHY AS SMEARING BLOOD ON THE DOORWAY

"

AND THE WORLD HAS WATCHED, MESMERIZED

Glamour burns through language, religious, and cultural barriers. Without any conscious intention to delve into magic, the South Korean entertainment industry has harnassed glamour on an unprecedented scale.

For any witch setting down their path, if you want to understand ritual, there is no better place to start than a playlist of BTS videos.

RITUALS NEED GLAMOUR

Why do we do magic ritual? Because we want to create a new timeline, a new reality, a new perspective. We are impregnating ourselves with potential. Glamour magic is immediate and accessible, and with the ubiquity of the Internet, it has real potential to shift society on an international scale.

Culture is often called 'soft power' compared to the 'hard power' of heavy industry or the military. But this soft power is now poised as a threat to traditional regimes across the world, thanks to the multimedia whirl of online glamour.

But despite Kpop demonstrating its effectiveness, its strategies are ignored by modern witches. Too many rituals today are the equivalent of a beige couch, done without any swagger, without any aesthetic sense, any juicy pleasure. It's like watching a bunch of people with no rhythm trying to dance.

Ignoring the inherent sensuality of the human body leads to half-effective rituals. After all, it is our body that leads us into rituals, and our body that revels in the results. The operator of the ritual is not a discombobulated brain - they are a witch with a powerful physical form.

RUBEDO

THE FIRST SPELL I EVER DID WAS
FOR MONEY.

AS A NEW WITCH, I WATCHED THE
NOTORIOUS DISINFO CON TALK
BY OCCULTIST AND COMIC BOOK
WRITER GRANT MORRISON, IN WHICH
THEY GAVE THEIR FORMULA FOR
CREATING A SIGIL.

THEY DREW ONE ON THEIR CHEST
AND CHARGED IT WITH THE EXTREME
FEAR AND ADRENALINE OF
BUNGEE JUMPING.

I decided to start a bit smaller. I drew a sigil on my hand, then went to an amusement park outside of Seoul, so I could charge it while riding the T Express.

I'm deathly afraid of heights and the T Express is the ninth-fastest, fourth-tallest, and third-longest wooden roller coaster in the entire world.

But lo and behold, in just a few hours, I had a significant, totally unexpected sum of money in my bank account.

> **WHEN YOU SHIFT YOUR MINDSET, YOU SHIFT YOUR REALITY**

A warning here: don't go chasing extremes recklessly. Use your common sense. If your gut says it's unsafe, heed that advice. But a ritual's efficacy, in my experience, heightens when the ritual is more intense. After all, when you shift your mindset, you shift your reality.

Magic often puts people off because it has a reputation for being too extra. It's notorious for requiring torture, death, and rare items that will absolutely land you in prison. Even the word 'scapegoat' comes from the ancient Yom Kippur ritual of symbolically placing the sins of the people on a sweet, innocent goat, which is then sent out into the blazing desert to die.

What if you don't want to ingest handfuls of psilocybin mushrooms, sacrifice virgin maidens on an altar, or take part in an orgy? What if rollercoasters scare you too much? Do you need to choose between high-risk and high-result rituals?

Thanks to immersive modern technology, we may not need to anymore.

NEW MEDIUMS

Media theorist Marshall McLuhan famously said that the medium is more influential than the actual message. He was talking about communication on things like radio, newspapers, and television back in the 1960s. But this idea that the medium determines the message applies deftly to magical ritual as well; after all, it's also a technology for communication.

The medium, or the magic circle, is often overlooked in magic. But it is the container in which rituals take place, and it can either fertilize the message or drain its energy. An Instagram Reel is going to dramatically lose effectiveness if printed inside a paper magazine.

A hunting ritual inside a dark cave, whose floor is covered with the skulls of paleolithic bears, is a different medium than an air-conditioned apartment in New York City with your nine other roommates. These days, most of us don't have easy access to a wild forest to go dance naked in — we live in a very different context.

So what becomes of our magic circles as we increasingly share all the spaces we pass through: the rides we take, our offices, our gardens, and our crowded apartments? How do you perform a successful ritual as it gets harder and harder to feel like our mediums are magical?

We update the medium.

CYBORG

cy·borg
/ˈsīˌbôrg/
noun

A person whose physical abilities are extended beyond normal human limitations by mechanical elements built into the body.

Humans have always looked for ways to augment their bodies with technology. The long wands used by occultists were an extension of their finger, an antenna directing energy.

Now, those wands are smartphones, which cycle energy between individuals and the collective conscious of the Internet. Many of us are attached to ours 24/7.

You might want to argue that there's a large difference between an iPhone and those occultists' wands. But as Amber Case, cyber anthropologist, has said, smartphones bend space and time. 'Everyone [is] carrying around wormholes in their pockets.'

This level of connection with technology isn't new either. Neither is the idea of cyborgs – just look at the alchemy sci-fi masterpiece *Frankenstein*.

Since Mary Shelley, science fiction has turned into science fact, as pacemakers have been implanted into our chests, artificial hands with articulate and pressure-sensitive fingers affixed to our wrists.

Artist Neil Harbisson, who is completely color blind, has an antenna-like implant in his skull, which vibrates to help him differentiate between different color wavelengths, including UV, which the human eye normally can't see. Perhaps, in the future, a witch will have a similar implant that measures electrical energy, which will help her see how much energy her rituals whip up.

Some witches don't like this. A lot of modern magic fetishizes nature and disavow machines, and modern technology, as 'unnatural.'

Meanwhile, magic is the least 'natural' thing of all – you, the operator, are breaking the laws of physics to compel the Universe to align with your True Will. Just because you're using herbs and crystals doesn't make magic 'natural' any more than using soy sauce makes a dish authentically Asian.

During an interview with *The Guardian*, burlesque dancer Dita Von Teese said, 'I enjoy walking the streets of Paris and looking at all the man-made beauty ... more than I like being on the beach in California. I feel like glamour is ... the creation of art and the creation of beauty.'

> **" MAGIC IS THE LEAST 'NATURAL' THING OF ALL "**

For me, it's the artificiality – the man-made aspects – that help remind me most of the occult body, because the artificial is a reminder of the human mind's agency. We are taking matters into our own hands.

The ultimate technology right now is the portable, ancestral altar of the *Homo cyborg*, augmented by the wand of the collective conscious: right now, the smartphone ... in the future, virtual reality headsets and implants.

THESE MAY LOOK LIKE OCULUS
HEADSETS, GOOGLE GLASSES, OR
INEVITABLY, IMPLANTS IN OUR
HEADS. WHATEVER FORM
THEY TAKE, THESE MACHINE
EXTENSIONS WILL CHANGE
HOW WE EXPERIENCE
THE PHYSICAL WORLD
AND ALLOW US TO
ENTER A NEW ONE:

THE METAVERSE.

METAVERSE

IN RITUAL, THE

MEDIUM IS

IDEALLY BOTH

A PHYSICAL

AND NON-

PHYSICAL PLACE.

SOMETHING

LIMINAL.

Smartphones can already create augmented reality, like 'Pokémon Go' and Snapchat filters: this is a digital reality, overlaid on top of the physical. But you're holding up a phone to your face, viewing the filter on its screen. The experience still feels like a clunky appendage of everyday life.

But one day, your cyborg self will be able to instantly slip in and out of a virtual world – this is the metaverse.

You can think of the metaverse as the Internet in 4-dimensional Technicolor. Movies like *Inception* and *The Matrix* explored themes of physical selves plugging into a dream/virtual world.

We're not quite there yet. Currently, the metaverse is still nascent, kind of like where the World Wide Web was at in 1997. But VR cyborg technology for the human body is advancing, and even as early as 2030, quantum computers may have the awe-inspiring power to create a next-level digital experience.

In this metaverse, there won't be physical laws, only the algorithm. In this sense, it will be like the most immersive, interactive, full-body 3D video game you could imagine. This is why Facebook, Microsoft, and other large companies are scrambling to become the leaders in this emerging dimension: the metaverse is the new frontier, and will soon be the ultimate reality.

Our cyborg extensions will let us move seamlessly between the digital and the physical/IRL (though I prefer the term AFK, 'away from keyboard,' used by cyber artist Legacy Russell in *Glitch Feminism*). We will have an extended digital identity – sometimes multiple fluid identities, perhaps similar to the characters in *Black Mirror*'s 'San Junipero.'

BUT WHAT DOES
THE METAVERSE
MEAN FOR
WITCHCRAFT?

Well, as those avatars, you will be able to perform high-stakes rituals, no virgin sacrifice needed. Perhaps, instead of riding the T Express, we'll be able to dive off a metaverse cliff with even better results, all the while perfectly safe from physical harm.

In the metaverse, your coven could be global. If there had been a fully mature metaverse at the time, #hextrump would have been like an in-person, AFK rally, with thousands of witches around the globe, gathered together. Imagine the power of those spells.

And not just the everyday spells. You could fly if you wanted to. You could spew fire from your mouth. You could virtually conjure up the spirit of Hekate, instead of trying to abstractly visualize her. She would appear in front of you, looking as 'real' as your digital hand.

Ancient spells that required the sacrifice of live animals will be humane inside the metaverse. Orgies can happen without sexually transmitted disease, or even other people. And who says the metaverse world needs to obey gravity? Or that our avatars should only have two arms and legs?

These extreme rituals may be tempered by new ethical concerns (is virtual murder acceptable?), but the potential for new permutations and experiments in ritual is mind-boggling.

WHAT IS A HIGH-PERFORMING RITUAL?

For new witches, magic ritual should result in observable change in the external world so that you can build confidence in your technique – not as a test of faith, but because of actual results.

Joseph McMoneagle, one of the people trained by the US government as a psychic spy for project STARGATE, said that no spy, aka 'remote viewer,' was ever 100 percent accurate. Instead, 70 percent was considered a high-performer. So, I've unscientifically assigned 70 percent as my standard.

I personally use a spreadsheet to list all my rituals. This is not to pressure myself. Instead, if my cumulative success rate dips below 60 percent, I immediately know that I need to start analyzing and revamping rituals, because something isn't working.

You are under no obligation to tell anyone about your success rate. In fact, most of the time, you want to work in silence, without anyone having any clue when you're doing rituals.

Important note: have a general idea of what a reasonable timeframe looks like. Some rituals' results come to pass, but they take too long. I would consider such spells technically unsuccessful; reasonable timeframes are essential.

When caves were an effective medium to facilitate hyped-up magic ritual, our ancestors created wall animations. In the 19th century, some of the earliest films depicted fictional occult rituals, deeply impacting how witches have practiced magic since.

And now, there is a new medium – the burgeoning metaverse – where the moving picture is developing into an interactive, immersive experience, which can be participated in by people all around the world.

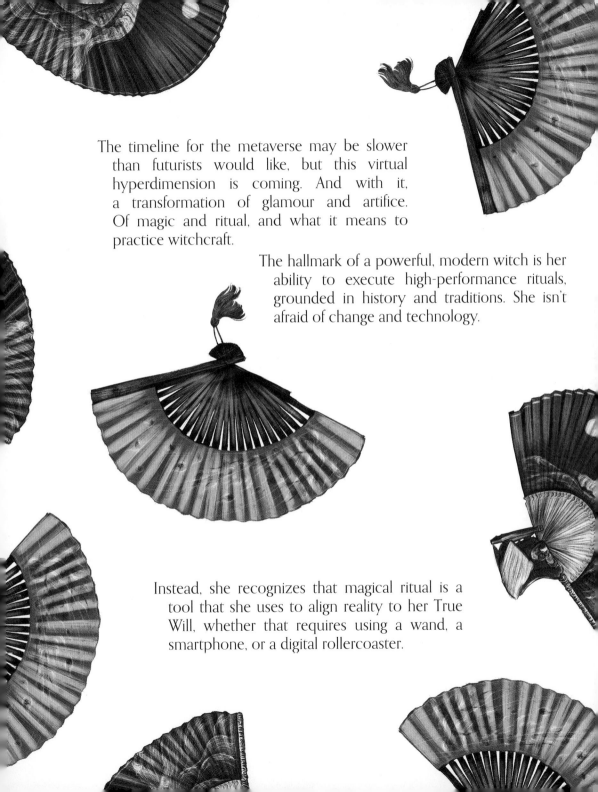

The timeline for the metaverse may be slower than futurists would like, but this virtual hyperdimension is coming. And with it, a transformation of glamour and artifice. Of magic and ritual, and what it means to practice witchcraft.

The hallmark of a powerful, modern witch is her ability to execute high-performance rituals, grounded in history and traditions. She isn't afraid of change and technology.

Instead, she recognizes that magical ritual is a tool that she uses to align reality to her True Will, whether that requires using a wand, a smartphone, or a digital rollercoaster.

EARTH · EARTH

土

E A

R

T H

土

EARTH · EARTH · EARTH · EARTH · EARTH · EARTH · EARTH ·

NIGREDO

IN SOUTH KOREA, THE TWO BIGGEST
HOLIDAYS ARE SEOLLAL 설날 (LUNAR
NEW YEAR) AND CHUSEOK 추석
(KOREAN THANKSGIVING).

ON BOTH DAYS, THE COUNTRY SHUTS
DOWN AND MILLIONS OF FAMILIES
PERFORM ANCESTRAL VENERATION
RITES, OR *JESA* 제사, THEY LAY OUT
A TABLE OF FOOD AND ALCOHOL,
ALONG WITH PICTURES AND
NAMEPLATES OF THE ANCESTORS, TO
HONOR AND REMEMBER THEM.

My first *jesa* 제사, was in the early 2000s, when I traveled to Korea for a semester in college. In some families, *jesa* 제사 is a complicated and elaborate affair, with the women spending days preparing food to present to the ancestors.

In my family, it's a smaller ceremony: a less involved, but still delicious table of food and alcohol is offered to the departed. We acknowledge their memory, and then our ancestors, in turn, bless our offerings. At the end, we sit and eat.

Outside of Korea, this scene is less common. In the Western world, food and other offerings are an often overlooked part of magic, perhaps because of the modern assumption that the material world isn't as important as 'energy.' But in Asia, ATRs (African traditional religions), and non-Westernized communities, food and alcohol are thought to literally feed the spirit.

Just as we break bread with respected guests, offering food in rituals is an accessible and nourishing way to get closer to your magic.

EVERYDAY MAGIC
OF COOKING

In many monastaries, Buddhist monks sit and chant all day: this meditation is viewed as the ideal form of attaining enlightenment.

But what about the cooks, who make sure the rice is free of stone, delicious to eat, cooked with care, not burnt? That is also meditation, and yet it is often disregarded by Western acolytes; food is too body-based, cooking too mundane. Besides, this is kitchen stuff – the realm of femininity.

But as Jeong Kwan, a Buddhist nun, says on *Chef's Table*, 'There is no difference between cooking and pursuing Buddha's way.'

The magic of food and cooking is potent, and not only for ceremonies like *jesa* 제사. You can find this magic when you're baking a pie, or grilling a steak. Magic doesn't just happen when you're doing a candle spell or sitting on a cushion in lotus position.

As Jeong Kwan says, 'By making soy sauce, I am reliving the wisdom of my ancestors ... I see my grandmother, my mother, the elders in the temple, and me.'

I can't overemphasize enough, for baby witches, the importance of giving yourself enough avenues for magic to come through.

If ritual is overly precious and only happens during special times, then you've unintentionally pigeonholed magic as separate, different, and 'out there.' Instead, you want magic to become an everyday part of your life: to have your spells be a foregone conclusion, as real as the burrito you're about to eat.

> **" THERE IS NO DIFFERENCE BETWEEN COOKING AND PURSUING BUDDHA'S WAY "**

I love to incorporate food into my magic as dinner offerings for the spirits I work with.

JUPITER OFFERINGS

While it's true that spirits don't need sustenance like us biological humans, you still want to 'feed' your rituals. The witch is constantly nourishing the oft-invisible worlds of chthonic, nature, and celestial spirits, and the dead. While the energy you offer does also feed them, literal food can add an extra potency.

Physical offerings are often the missing link for new witches who are diligently performing rituals but who have poor results. Maybe they have dream after dream where their magic intentions play out. But without the material touchstone of a physical offering, the results stay in la la land.

I find this to be especially true when doing money magic, where I need very grounded results. After all, no landlord will accept a rent check from the astral realm.

So, after petitioning the spirit of Jove for extra money, I offer a nice pork chop with a side of roasted potatoes, setting it out with a small glass of Johnny Walker Blue. This is not the time for fast food. This is a spread I'd serve any well-heeled guest: Jove is, after all, a fabulously wealthy god who I'm asking nicely for money.

Whether it's pork chops, vegan cheese, or a bag of Flamin' Hot Cheetos, food feeds your spell and builds the energy for a petition. I wouldn't say that elaborate offerings are necessary, but it's important that they're spiritually nourishing. Large volumes of empty offerings are just as bad as large volumes of junk food for your body.

And always remember: there is something about physically touching and, especially, preparing something, which really affects one psychologically. A good rule of thumb; the more 'real' the ritual feels, the more successful it is. And because food is so foundational to this reality, it's much more substantial than a 'so mote it be' or a hand gesture. The offerings are a tangible reason for the spirits, or whatever you want to call it, to come to be.

HEKATE OFFERINGS

Jove isn't the only deity I offer food to. During the New Moon, I prepare a traditional Deipnon dinner of hardboiled eggs, honey, and wine for Hekate — a popular dark goddess for witches, who has had something of a renaissance in the past couple of decades alongside other dark goddesses like Lilith.

I do my best to use good-quality eggs and local honey and, as tradition dictates, I offer the food but I don't eat it. I keep it on my Hekate altar, until I feel that she has taken her fill.

This is not an elaborate Deipnon feast, and this is on purpose. To me, the archetype of Jove is Jay-Z, cruising on a yacht in the "Big Pimpin'" video; Hekate, not so much. She isn't impressed by pomp, and prefers the simple and practical.

For regular rituals like the New Moon, it's better to stay small than to start big and then scale back. Establish a minimum to stick to. This is not because Hekate will get offended, but because your own guilt might get in the way. If you have fancier Deipnon some months, while others scrape the barrel, it's easy to feel like your work with Hekate is reduced during those leaner months.

This is also why I give Jove a shot glass of Johnny Walker Blue, instead of a tumbler; it'll feel less prosperous if I have to cut back on this expensive liquor, which would affect my spell work. I want to maintain a sustainable minimum, which works just fine. If I have an absolutely out-of-the-ordinary request, then, and only then, is it worth the extra expense to splurge.

COOKING AS ALCHEMY

In the recent past, starvation was commonplace, food a precious offering. Now we live in a world where most of us will not starve to death; if anything, we're more likely to die from too much food.

And yet, in today's world, there is endless hunger: people eating processed foods with little nutrition, giving offerings with unfocused energy. We eat endlessly without feeling satiated – what sort of bounty and comfort are we looking for?

When I lived in Bali, I went to a New Moon ritual at a local temple where we were given uncooked grains of rice to put on our forehead and under our tongue. The whole day, I didn't physically eat, and yet I felt zero hunger. I was so spiritually full.

My appetite was transformed into sublimated satiety.

Before modern chemistry, there was alchemy, which has been portrayed in popular culture as a pseudo-science dedicated to turning base lead to precious gold. However, the tradition's texts were written in code, meant only to be fully understood by those looking deeper.

Those like the witch.

Alchemy, true alchemy, isn't just about material transformation. Alchemy helps us view life's deepest lessons through material objects. After all, the same herb can be a poison or a healing tonic, depending on who is making the elixir.

As the Hermetic principles state: as above, so below. As you transform the lead by boiling, fermenting, and turning it to ash, you transform your soul, leeching out the impurities: rarifying the metal of your mind by reconstructing the 'real' materials in your hands.

In cooking, you take the motions of your body, the energy of your hands and, over fire, you create a manna that sustains your body – the altar of your ancestor's DNA. When you feed yourself, you feed them as well.

COOKING
AND FOOD MAY SEEM
HUMDRUM, BUT THEY ARE
ALCHEMY PAR EXCELLENCE. THE POT
BOILING WITH KOREAN KIMCHI
STEW IS AS POWERFUL
AS A SHAKESPEAREAN
CAULDRON BOILING
EYE OF NEWT.

ALBEDO

RIGHT NOW, IF I LOOK TO MY LEFT,
I CAN SEE 'BOB'. BOB IS A CLEAR
CRYSTAL THAT I BOUGHT ON ETSY.

I WANTED TO RUN AN EXPERIMENT,
TO SEE IF CRYSTALS HAD ANY SORT OF
OBSERVABLE EFFECT ON MY MAGIC.

The results of my very unscientific experiment were mixed. Bob didn't affect my ritual's results per se, but he did bring a sense of beauty, and maybe even additional focus.

But Bob didn't pirouette into my room out of thin air. I paid shipping from Europe. And he didn't just appear in that Etsy store as a shiny, cut crystal. Bob was a rock that spent thousands of years under the ground, growing and living in what witch-geologist Kathleen Borealis calls 'geological time.' This is not just centuries or even millennia. This is eons. Maybe since the Earth's beginning, Bob has always been there.

He is a reminder to me that there exists something deeper than human time: magical, liminal time.

I have created an entire mythology around Bob and his kind. This is how material becomes significant and magical – you imbue it with meaning. Without the myth, a crystal is just a shiny bauble.

This is what sympathetic magic is built upon – adding layers of meanings into your ritual, with the aid of material offerings.

You will often see witches casting a love spell on Friday, using the color green and rose petals – this is because Friday is Venus' day, green is Venus' color, and roses are associated with love. These witches are building 'sympathy' by adding coat after coat of the desired message.

WHEN CHOSEN WISELY,
CRYSTALS AND OTHER
MATERIAL CAN BE AN
EXCELLENT WAY TO
GROUND THE MAGIC,
AND THE RESULTS, IN
THIS REALITY.

MATERIA MAGICAE

Magic practitioners have often been obsessed with exotic, rare items. Occult texts are notorious for requiring things akin to tiger pelts or 'cut out' a magic circle. Physical offerings can add that extra oomph to a ritual, because they require so much effort to procure. Your mind registers it as: you must really, really want this magical result. But they continued their religion and magic practices by developing hoodoo, with the flora and fauna of the New World. Cunning folk in all cultures have always made do with whatever materials were readily available. When African slaves were brought over to the Americas, they lost the plants and materials of their homeland. However, folk magic has shown us that you don't need rare items from far away: when a tree struck not once, not twice, but three times by lightning. There's definitely a certain delight in using a heavy, ivory-handled dagger to wood from a tree struck

THE FUTURIST WITCH WANTS TO

BRING MAGIC FROM 'OUT THERE' –

FROM THE REALM OF IMAGINATION

– INTO THE EVERYDAY 'HERE' OF

EMBODIED LIFE. EXOTIC ITEMS

ARE JUST ONE TOOL OF MANY, NOT

THE BE-ALL AND END-ALL. A TOOL'S

MOST IMPORTANT CHARACTERISTIC

IS ITS SIGNIFICANCE TO YOU.

 INCENSE

In the 'Greek Magical Papyri' – the working notebook of a Hellenistic Egyptian sorcerer – smells are an important material part of rituals.

Olfactory advice appears across other Western occult texts. If you want to follow it, and introduce scent into your magic, you can use the obvious materials: incense or resins. But you can also use charred meat; it seems many baneful and chaotic spirits love the hellish smell of burning protein.

I never fully understood the whole incense thing, until Dr. Cyndi Brannen, of the Hekate blog *Keeping Her Keys*, told me that burning incense can change the atmosphere. From a spiritual point of view, you're releasing materials from their solid form into a more airy, spirit-based one. And from a physical point of view, it can also release chemicals; incensole acetate, found in frankincense, has been found to ease anxiety and lift moods.

The Oracles of Delphi, who were famous for being the psychic mouthpieces of the gods, were getting high. *National Geographic* wrote of 'evidence of [sweet-smelling] hallucinogenic gases rising from a nearby spring and preserved within the [Delphi] temple rock.'

But it's about more than sparking up: don't underestimate the smoke as a terrific way to add ambience. I use multiple incense sticks during rituals, because the smoky haze makes it easier to imagine spirits. The shape of the smoke, the airy nature – these add to the overall theater.

SMOKE CLEANSING

✦

We've all seen videos of witches waving around a bundle of dried white sage to cleanse a space. However, there are varieties of plant-life that can provide just as effective smoke cleansing.

David Borji Shi, the Manchu-Chinese-American author of *North Asian Magic*, has written about how marsh labrador is commonly used among Amur Siberians, and Asian thyme by Manchus. Juniper is a solid choice for those of Northeast Asian ancestry, such as Korean, Mongolian, and Manchu-Chinese. Those with Northern European ancestry may find that their elders also used juniper, due to a similar climate.

Shi relays these tips from shaman elders about which plants to use:

1. Herbs that the person's direct ancestors used in a sacred way
2. Herbs that grow locally/indigenously where the person is based

For example, white sage grows mainly in the California region of America, so if you live in Florida, it would be worth looking into local plants.

OVER-MATERIALISM

A lot of modern magic tries to do away with materials, or diminishes their magical powers. After all, everything emanates from the mind, so why bring in the dense, gross material stuff like food, which can rot?

Of course, there's also the flip side of this 'energy only' mindset: materialism. Crystals and incense are over-mined and over-harvested, and buying them in mass quantities means your magic is impotent. When you approach materials with a consumerist mindset, they don't have real significance beyond the dip of your bank balance

It's one thing if everyone is using Frankincense with deep reverence and respect, but too many witches are just buying it in bulk and using it willy nilly. They might as well be burning cash instead. Like popping diet pills expecting some miracle weight-loss method, this approach to magic ignores the holistic nature of ritual, from the shadow work to the glamour that helps shift our mindset.

> **THIS IS CONSUMER MAGIC. DIET MAGIC. ASPARTAME MAGIC.**

This is Consumer Magic. Diet Magic. Aspartame Magic.

As long as we have a body with its cocktail of hormones and senses, our materials serve a real purpose. They ground our rituals and give them meaning.

'PURE' MAGIC MATERIALS

But overconsumption isn't our only sin. A lot of witches are purists: they only want to use traditional materials to stay historically accurate in their spells.

This type of witchcraft is about having the right crystals and herbs, and mixing those together in some sort of cauldron. This is romantic, but how many of us are privy to the wilds of the forest? Or do we order our herbs off of Amazon and Etsy?

Witches of yore did things out of necessity. They utilized the nature around them, and we need to acknowledge the reality of what surrounds us today: the trash and plastics and pollution.

The Earth is traumatized, and yet an alarming number of witches, especially in pagan communities, are in denial. They want to cling to the idealized fantasy of virginal wilds, pure and untouched, unfingered by human hands.

My crystal, Bob, for all I know, was forced out from the ground. Someone reached inside the womb of Mother Earth and ripped Bob out, without his consent. The disconnect between the Etsy shop and my doorstep doesn't erase the real story. If crystals are conductors of energy, then what about all the humans who handled Bob, all their dreams and traumas? Did their energy also lodge inside him?

And what about your incense? So many plants today are genetically altered, or at the very least use chemical pesticides. How does that affect your ritual? And as honeybees die at alarming rates, and are less available to pollinate wild flora, what sort of plants will you burn in their stead?

This is why I find folk magic intriguing. The materials are whatever you have on hand – Pine-Sol cleaner to wash floors during ritual, a handmade poppet stuffed with your desired one's hair, a ziplock bag of spell water in the freezer. Personally, I like using DNA – saliva, blood, hair, fingernail clippings.

Even without telling you exactly what these materials would do, you can probably already guess their purpose. Would you want squeaky clean floors for something more akin to a love or a banishing spell? Would you put someone's hair in a doll because you had zero interest in them?

I find one of the most magical mindsets is animism, where we see spirit in everything around us, including inanimate objects. This already adds a base layer of significance, when the rock, the incense, the bowl of rice offered, has a myth to it.

And these myths are not static monoliths.

A safety pin can either be a humdrum tailoring item to keep clothes together … or it can be a fashion statement of a skater kid. Vaseline can be an innocent salve for chapped lips … or used as lubricant. Menstrual blood can be something to dread each month … or a powerful ingredient to add in a spell for sex.

Ultimately, you are the one who decides what significance to put into the materials. You have the agency.

HOW TO DO OFFERINGS

✧

Occultist Jason Miller is a frequent guest on my YouTube channel and teacher of the popular online course, 'Sorcery of Hekate.' He writes on sorcery and is ordained as a *Ngakpa* – a type of Buddhist Tantric monk.

Q1: You've mentioned that, if a witch is vegan and doesn't want to offer eggs during Deipnon, they can offer white cakes instead. But the results will not be same. This freaks out out a lot of witches because they think this means the results will be worse. Would you explain what you mean by 'not the same?'

A: It's very difficult to apprehend almost anything without instantly judging it to be better or worse. Let's take the example of a grilled cheese sandwich. If you don't have butter in the house, you can make it with mayonnaise on the outside of the bread. Is this good or bad? Depends on what you want, but ultimately we don't have to declare one better or worse – just understand how they differ and accept reality as it is.

Tibetans decided that they were not going to offer blood sacrifice to spirits that were used to it in the past. They devised cakes called tormas that are blood red in color and sometimes mimic internal organs … some say it's better, some say it's worse. I say that even that is not nuanced enough of a view, because different spirits may have different views on it, different tormas are made different ways, etc.

Q2: When are visualization-only offerings effective? For example, is there a time when it may be even more effective than actually giving physical offerings?

A: If you keep a regular practice and have a good relationship with the spirits you are working with, sometimes you can do just a visualized offering but, even if I can't give anything physical, I rub my hands together and link it to the heat emanating from them.

For large ceremonies, you might want to go bigger on the physical offerings. I have been to ceremonies where there is great expense in creating a delightful display of offerings. You can [also offer] demanding physical activity like ritual flagellation.

Q3: What are some best practices, cross-culturally, that you've found?

Rather than cherry pick cross-culturally, let me just say that if you are not already in a tradition that prescribes offerings, you have a huge opportunity to shape the future. Animal sacrifice may be the tradition in a lot of the world, but if you live in the city or the suburbs and don't regularly kill animals for food, is this an appropriate thing to start doing? Maybe yes, maybe no, but it's a good time to evaluate the question.

Of course, if you are in a tradition, that doesn't mean that you must never change. Traditions are in a constant state of debate. You do, however, have more to worry about than just your own opinion. That's the beauty of a tradition — you have something to measure [yourself] against.

RUBEDO

WE HAVE FRANKINCENSE AND SINGLE
MALT WHISKEY HERE ON EARTH. BUT
WHAT SORT OF OFFERINGS WOULD
HUMANS GIVE IF WE LIVED ON THE
MOON? WHAT SORT OF RITUALS
WOULD WE PERFORM?

I SAW GLIMPSES OF THE ANSWER IN
2018, WHEN I WENT TO SEE ARTIST
JORGE MAÑES RUBIO'S EXHIBIT, *PEAK
OF ETERNAL LIGHT*, AT THE BARAKAT
SEOUL GALLERY.

Rubio,
the first resident artist at the
European Space Agency, envisioned
a massive observatory facing
beloved Earth. In this cathedral, a
high priestess would wear ceremonial
garb made of moondust and gold, one
of the main metals in spaceships.

As it would be expensive and
inefficient to bring heavy quartz
crystals, incense, and resins from Earth,
ritual materials would have to be lunar.
Moondust isn't made of the bones of
our ancestors, and the irradiated soil
can't grow any crops that we can eat.
But the soil would become empowered
in the hands of the spiritual leaders, who
would mold it into death masks that
honor the new lunar ancestors, the brave
souls who aided the colony in finding
water ice, the most valuable resource
for their survival.

For witches today, this is science
fiction. But as we exhaust Earth's
resources, space travel is inevitable. We
may have no choice but to terraform
other planets, as climate change
and pollution turn our home planet
inhospitable.

When this happens, what will
magic look like for the *Homo sapiens*
who leave the Chauvet Caves behind
for the coldest, darkest craters
of the Moon?

EARTH-NATURE MYTH

Earth is covered in alien materials. Rocks from space have always fallen to its surface, to our fascination and sometimes horror. Moldavite, a crystal that has renewed in popularity thanks to WitchTok, formed when an asteroid crashed in Central Europe 15 million years ago.

Yet many witches seem oblivious to outer space, forgetting that Earth is but a small part of our solar system, which itself is just a speck in the vastness of the Universe. Magic happens everywhere, not just on our planet.

Animism applies to everything, from the rocks to the farthest stars; Earth isn't the center of the Universe. Humans are a minuscule part of nature's reaches, as are the man-made objects that we've molded: nuclear power plants, plastic bottles, smartphones. In the same vein, non-Earth materials also have worthy spirits, even if they are utterly alien.

Hermetic occult philosophy famously states, 'That which is above is like to that which is below, and that which is below is like to that which is above,' a phrase that witches have often interpreted to mean that the physical and spiritual world reflect each other.

OUR ALIEN ANCESTORS

So many spiritual traditions are deeply invested in extraterrestrial mythology. Whether it's a sky god Hwanung 환웅 coming down to father the Korean people, or Genghis Khan and the Mongols speaking of Tengri, a sky god and creator of all things, many origin myths involve some celestial being starting a lineage down on Earth.

Indigenous people around the world believe they are descendants of an extraterrestrial race. For the Dogon people of West Africa, they believe they are from the Sirius star system. And so much of the concept of 'star seeds,' which has unfortunately been corrupted by modern New Age circles, was inspired by Indigenous American legends of alien ancestors and extraterrestrial contact.

In Hermetic philosophy, if you change something in the physical realm, e.g, give offerings, then there will be a corresponding change in the astral, and vice-versa. 'As above, so below' has often been quoted as the explanation of how sympathetic magic works.

However, the original phrase also has a literal meaning – the 'above' is the celestial origin of the 'below': all matter on Earth. In Hermeticism, 'God' is endless, omnipotent potential that lives beyond the stars. To materialize on Earth, whether as a human or raindrop or caterpillar, the essence of God filters through the seven 'wandering stars' in our solar system: the Sun, the Moon, Mercury, Venus, Mars, Jupiter, and Saturn.

There are Earth materials (like specific plants and rocks) that correspond to the seven planets. We utilize these materials as offerings in planetary magic, because their qualities are directly related to Venus or Mars or Jupiter.

Human beings contain all seven planets. To ignore this is to ignore our place in the Universe: our roots are incomplete without bringing in the alien and celestial.

"
OUR ROOTS ARE INCOMPLETE WITHOUT BRINGING IN THE ALIEN AND CELESTIAL
"

OUR MAGIC IS AS AT HOME ON THE MOON ...

...AS IT IS ON THE EARTH.

PRIMA MATERIA

MAGIC'S

UNIVERSAL

POTENTIAL

IS

ALCHEMIC.

According to alchemy, all things begin as *prima materia*, which is the formless, raw starting material for matter. In Hermeticism, and many other origin myths, we can also see it as a particularly fluid aspect of God.

Nineteenth-century author Mary Anne Atwood described it as 'a certain pure matter, which, being discovered and brought by art to perfection, converts to itself proportionally all imperfect bodies that it touches.'

Prima materia starts off without form, but by interacting with human imagination and ingenuity, it manifests, harmoniously adding itself to the world.

To me, this sounds like what offerings are at their core: something that, through layers of myth and narrative, take on significance. This significance then gives it the power to sympathetically correspond to our True Will.

Folk magic around the world is based on this very premise – that you work with what you've got, and build new mythologies to replace those that can't be sustained.

For the witch, this means that we don't have to hold on to every relic.

That we are free to start building new myths.

That the future shouldn't scare us.

"

THE
ULTIMATE
MATERIA
MAGICA IS YOU

"

Physical offerings help ground our magic, but they are a means to an end, not the actual end itself. While they ground our magic in its beginnings, the ultimate materia magica is you.

According to modern alchemist Avery Hopkins, *"Alchemy is the understanding of the relationship between consciousness and matter ... If alchemy is at all an 'art of transformation' it is one that understands how consciousness creates and transforms itself into matter."*

For our magic to continue to expand, we need to let go of the unsustainable past. As we all journey into the future, you don't want to be limited by the illusion that it's the crystal or incense that powers your magic, when it all comes from you: your body, your mind, and your True Will.

Even now, on Earth, we'll find ourselves in situations where we don't have the time or ability to give physical offerings. And the fact is, these may be some of the most powerful rituals we experience — the moments where we fall on our knees, our palms empty but full of humility. I sometimes joke and call it a 'Jesus take the wheel moment,' but offering your trust and surrender to the mysterious can often yield miracles.

E   M   P   T

I N E S S

Eastern esotericism teaches us that, ultimately, all the things we think of as solid are actually an illusion. Around us is just emptiness.

In *chöd* meditation, the original Tibetan meditation that Feeding Your Demons™ is based on, you offer a visualization of your chopped-up body as food for spirits. Part of the guest list are demons, to whom you willingly offer yourself up as an especially gruesome, bloody sacrifice. This meditation is traditionally done in frightening places, like a literal charnel or cremation grounds, where you are surrounded by actual rotting corpses.

According to Dr. Ben Joffe, anthropologist of Tibet and Tibetan translator, 'the reason you simulate your own violent death, and you willingly offer up that idea of self to demons, is because you are cutting (that's what *chöd* means: severing) your attachment to the idea that the body that you perceive from moment to moment is something fixed and permanent. Through your offering, you realize that your physical body and sense of self is really more an idea ... less substantial than you think.'

" THIS MEDIATION IS TRADITIONALLY DONE IN FRIGHTENING PLACES "

The implications of chöd are profound for a witch.

Even though you haven't literally cut up your physical flesh,

the ritualized visualization provides real sustenance to the spirits.

And at the end of the meditation, after the spirits have had their fill,

you 'dissolve' the feast, including all the guests.

As you do, you realize that even the most frightening demons are

both as real and unreal as you are.

We exist in a physical sense, but on a deeper level,

we are created by our minds.

It's the same with all physical materials.

This doesn't negate the practical value of physical offerings.

However, if the materials become the focus,

to the detriment of a witch's results and wallet,

she forgotten that the materials are a conduit, not the source.

The Emerald Tablet (a 3,000-year-old Western alchemy text) and *Rig Veda* (a 6,000-year-old Indian text) both speak of how the knower - the observer - is the bridge between the infinity of the divine, and the finite of the material world.

As a witch, don't limit yourself to the past, or to the Earth. The entire Universe is at your disposal, if you reach out farther.

Of course, it helps to start out small with things like cooking: an offering to the altar of the physical body, or with materials like crystals and incense that help to further ground our True Will.

But as we look to the stars, we release ourselves from the illusion of limits.

Will witchcraft on the Moon be the same as on Earth? Probably not. But different results are not necessarily worse. They're just different. Remember that it is the significance that we attach to the offering, not the material itself, that all the mojo comes from.

Ultimately, offerings are a symbol of our intentions for our True Will - its true power transcends solidity. Just like the word 'magic' can't fully contain all its multitudes, offerings are simply pointers to the sprawling expanse of your experience and self.

Our True Will conjoins with the *prima materia*, ready to be expressed.

METAL

금金

METAL

NIGREDO

I WAS A PRE-TEEN IN THE HEYDAY OF
PSYCHIC HOTLINE INFOMERCIALS,
INCLUDING MISS CLEO'S. IT'S A
GOOD THING I WAS TOO YOUNG
TO ACTUALLY CALL – I WOULD HAVE
GONE BROKE ASKING ABOUT MY
SCHOOLGIRL CRUSHES.

EVEN AS A YOUNG ATHEIST, I STILL
WANTED TO BELIEVE THAT THERE
WAS SOME OMNIPOTENT FORCE OUT
THERE THAT COULD GIVE ME A
PLAY-BY-PLAY OF MY LIFE.

Whether you call it fortune-telling, or something more fancy like divination, human beings are control freaks about the future. In ancient China, 'May you live in interesting times' was an actual curse. Unpredictability was – and is – seen as chaos, and chaos is scary for most people.

BUT THE WITCH IS NOT MOST PEOPLE.

WE MOVE WITH CURIOSITY, NOT FEAR, AS WE TURN THE CORNERS.

WE ARE NOT VICTIMS TO LIFE'S VICISSITUDES.

We don't analyze the stars or read tarot cards out of fear. A witch doesn't practice divination with white-knuckle, sweaty-brow anxiety about 'interesting times.'

INSTEAD, SHE IS AN ACTIVE, EVEN PLAYFUL PARTICIPANT IN SHAPING HER FUTURE AND ALIGNING IT TO HER TRUE WILL.

THEY WERE ANIMISTS WHO BELIEVED THE NATURAL WORLD WAS FULL OF CLUES ABOUT WHAT WAS TO COME ✦ THEY WERE ANIMISTS WHO BELIEVED THE NATURAL WORLD WAS FULL OF CLUES ABOUT WHAT WAS TO COME ✦ THEY WERE ANIMISTS WHO BELIEVED THE NATURAL WORLD WAS FULL OF CLUES ABOUT WHAT WAS TO COME ✦ THEY WERE ANIMISTS WHO BELIEVED THE NATURAL WORLD WAS FULL OF CLUES ABOUT WHAT WAS TO COME ✦ THEY WERE ANIMISTS WHO BELIEVED THE NATURAL WORLD WAS FULL OF CLUES ABOUT WHAT WAS TO COME ✦

ASTROLOGY

Divination has been a part of human culture from its start. Of course, our ancestors didn't have Miss Cleo; instead, they utilized everything around them for fortune telling because they were animists who believed the natural world was full of clues about what was to come.

How the tea leaves tangled in the cup ... the way the wax dripped as the candle burned down ... the words that popped out in a book ... These were all prophetic. I'm sure there were quite a few ancestors who looked at human waste for divination as well.

Throughout history and different cultures, certain tools have risen or fallen out of fashion. Currently, astrology and tarot are the most popular. And as a baby witch, it's natural to be introduced to a shallow version of these tools through pop culture.

However, it's a shame to not learn the deeper techniques. Divination is so incredibly rich and constructive if studied sincerely. But most people don't know how 'Baby, what's your sign?' came to be.

Modern pop astrology in the English-speaking world is mainly the doing of Alan Leo, a British astrologer and clever capitalist, who found a way to make money from subscription astrology services. To maximize profits, he made the Sun sign the main focus, instead of looking at all the planets.

At the time, the general public didn't know better. During the Renaissance, educated European men could take university classes on astrology but, by Alan Leo's time, the practice was seen as old-fashioned superstition, supplanted by science. By the 19th century, people were reading Charles Darwin, while ancient Western astrology texts, many of which were in Latin and Arabic, were locked away in private libraries, untranslated.

It wasn't until the 1990s, thanks to Project Hindsight, that many of those traditional astrological works were translated into English. For the first time, these resources became readily available to a mass audience, rather than just the elite.

These traditional texts are a treasure trove of thousands of years of ancestral knowledge, from a time when astrology and astronomy were one and the same.

In the great civilizations around the ancient world, astrologers were amongst the most educated. Across Egypt, India, Persia, and the fertile crescent of the Middle East, an elite class of Star Priests spent a lifetime working through complicated math to predict transits, performing rituals to appease the stars and planets. Astrology was divine mathematics, a religious science, and the heavenly bodies were seen as gods who could bring fortune or calamity to the great emperors and caliphs and sultans.

Traditional astrology is based upon a cosmology in which the celestial bodies are powerful beings who you could work with magically. There is an entire mythology – an entire symphony – playing out in the sky. And while the astronomical math is important, that math is a tool to predict how the gods, i.e, the bodies in the sky, will influence life on Earth.

> **"**
> ## THE HEAVENLY BODIES WERE SEEN AS GODS WHO COULD BRING FORTUNE OR CALAMITY
> **"**

ASTROLOGY IS A NARRATIVE OF WHAT THOSE CELESTIAL GODS ARE DOING, AND WHEN THEY'LL MAKE MOVES. THIS MAKES IT A GREAT SCHEDULING TOOL FOR RITUALS; IF YOU KNOW HOW THE PLANETS WILL BE ALIGNED IN THE FUTURE, YOU CAN PREPARE AHEAD OF TIME.

ASTROLOGY EVOLVES

When traditional astrology was developed more than 4,000
    years ago, there were no schools of psychology. No
    sophisticated telescopes.
Astrology wasn't even for the common person; after all, if you
    were born into a family of farmers, you would be a farmer.
    If you were born as a woman, you were fated to marriage.
    There wasn't a lot of social mobility back then, and life was
    pretty much ordained.
Pre-modern astrology was mainly concerned with the flow of
    one's life and fortune based on external factors. Would you
    fall into poverty? Would your marriage produce children?
But feudal systems broke down and universities opened up to
    more people. As science developed in these schools, new
    planets and asteroids were discovered, and Freud and Jung
    helped develop modern psychology.

All these astrological branches have different techniques, and they all have merit depending on your needs. Debating that is pointless. A much more useful question to ask: what are you trying to accomplish? All these astrological branches have different techniques, and they all have merit depending on your needs. Debating that is pointless. A much more useful question to ask: what are you trying to accomplish? But as to whether traditional astrology, modern astrology, or specific schools are better? Debating that is pointless. A much more useful question to ask: what are you trying to accomplish? But as to whether traditional astrology, modern astrology, or specific schools are better? Like all dynamic systems, astrology has evolved alongside changes. Today, we have so many schools to choose from.

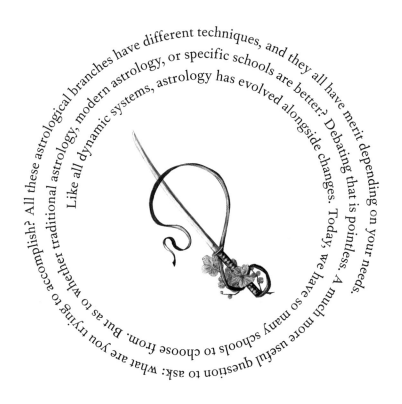

WHY ASTROLOGY MATTERS

Hands down, astrology is my go-to divination system —
especially for the big picture, when I'm considering long-
term time frames.

In *The Inner Sky*, a seminal modern astrology book, Steven
Forrest writes that a torrid love affair and a natal chart reading
will both offer you insight, but the latter is probably faster
and less painful (although both have their pros and cons).

This is why I always recommend that new witches get at least
three very in-depth birth chart readings from

01

A TRADITIONAL ASTROLOGER

02

A MODERN ASTROLOGER

03

A NON-WESTERN ASTROLOGER. FOR EXAMPLE, THIS COULD BE VEDIC (INDIAN) ASTROLOGY. I'M INTO *SAJU* 사주, WHICH IS KOREAN-STYLE ASTROLOGY, BASED UPON CHINA'S SYSTEM.

N O T E ✦ N O T E ✦ N O T E ✦ N O T E ✦ N O T E ✦ N O T E ✦ N O T E ✦ N O T E ✦

BIRTH TIMES

✦

You want to get your birth time as accurate as possible. Even a 15-minute gap can make a difference in readings. I personally don't have my birth certificate, so I've gone to several astrologers who specialize in chart rectification (finding your birth time).

Although this is an additional expense, I recommend that anyone who's unsure about their birth time go to more than one astrologer who specializes in rectification. This birth time will be used for the rest of your life, so it's worth the extra investment to make sure it's on point.

SCHEDULE
LIFE WITH
ASTROLOGY

✦

Overlaying any general transit over your specific birth chart is one of the most handy 'scheduling' tools when it comes to life.

Example: My natal chart has Gemini as the sign of my First House of self and body. Mercury Retrograde in Gemini will affect me differently than you, if your natal chart has Gemini in the Seventh House of other people (which is the opposite of the First House of self).

Magic rituals, in particular, can be extremely powerful when aligned with astrological timing.

Example: a love spell done on Friday, which is considered a Venusian day, during the hour of Venus is strategic, but doing it while the planet of Venus is exalted in the general transit *and* harmonious with aspects in your natal chart is especially fortuitous.

Once you have a clearer picture of what your birth chart says, you can move on to transit charts. These can be layered on top of each other, along with your birth charts; if my *saju* 사주 chart shows that the coming year will be better for certain projects, I overlay traditional Western astrology transit charts on top to see what part of the year is best for those undertakings.

Used together, charts are helpful for planning the future, like a weather forecast. Some days are windy: better for flying a kite. Others are going to be unseasonably hot, which means that you don't want to wear a heavy coat. Or, if you do want to wear that cute coat anyway, then you know to bring a cold drink and a sweatband.

Astrology is not about learning exactly what is going to happen. Instead, it's about having a general idea of the temperature and season your life is headed into, so you can adjust to meet the changes with grace.

TAROT

Of course, divination is not limited to astrology.

Cartomancy, which is divination that uses playing cards, tarot, Lenormand, oracle cards, and a number of other decks, has been popular in the Western world for centuries.

When it comes to the specifics of history, there's a lot of debate. For tarot, some say it is Egyptian, others claiming it as a Romani art. The most scholastically verifiable origin of tarot is that it started off as a card game, which soon evolved into fortune-telling.

But while the origins of cartomancy may be up for debate, it's an undeniably accessible tool. Unlike astrology, which requires complicated math, and used tools like an astrolabe in the past, cards have always been accessible to the everyday person.

These methods also serve different needs. While I find that astrology is great for long-term planning and more big-picture divination, cartomancy is extremely helpful for the short-term: anything that's three to six months in the future.

PLAYING CARDS VS. TAROT VS. LENORMAND VS. ORACLE CARDS

✧

All these decks can be used for cartomancy, although they have slightly different techniques.

Playing cards focus quite a lot on the cards' suits and numbers. I personally use them for very blunt 'yes-no' questions.

Tarot cards have many different styles. While the RWS deck is the most popular, there are older decks, like Marseille, which tend to have less illustrations. For tarot decks, I tend to use more open-ended questions like 'What is the energy around _____' for shadow work/introspective questions.

Lenormand cards tend to have more 'fixed' meanings, and I personally use them for practical matters where I want more straightforward answers.

Oracle cards have the meaning affixed right on the card. Typically, you pull out one card, and that is your message. These can be excellent for very young users; my toddler nephew has the 'Morning Calm' deck by Korean-American Seo Kelleher, which is about Korean spirituality.

If you want to simply feel safe and escape into fantasy, pop culture will give you the junk-food version of divination and consume your attention. It's no wonder that so many people see astrology and tarot as a scam.

Don't just learn from superficial astrology memes. If you want to align reality to your Will, you'll need to dive deeper.

But don't think that knowing everything about divination solves your life, either. Technically, you don't need any divination techniques to align reality. Astrology, tarot, and geomancy (my personal favorite) are just a set of tools, handled and interpreted by imperfect human beings. None of these tools make a person omniscient; remember, even a 70 percent rate is high-performing.

It's important to keep divination in perspective. Don't forget it is just a practical means to help you move through life with *noon chi* 눈치.

The whole point of divination is far more poignant than seeing the future; it's to survive, and hopefully thrive. Our ancestors developed divination techniques because they needed as much notice as they could get about whether they would be thrown out on the streets or starve to death.

These techniques and technologies exist because of our ancestors' desire to survive. Divination was created because of our ancestors' wish that their children and lineage would bloom.

T E C H N I Q U E
T E C H N I Q U E
T E C H N I Q U E

INTUITIVE VS. 'BOOK-LEARNED' TAROT TECHNIQUE

Intuitive card readers go by their personal feelings and interpretations of the symbols, while the book-learned go by the historically accepted meanings of the symbols.

These tips are from occultist Benebell Wen, author of *Holistic Tarot* and creator of the 'Spirit Keeper's Tarot':

How to do intuitive tarot readings well

1. Gaze at the imagery on the card and tap into your emotional response. Say, 'I see … '
2. Finish the sentence 'I feel … ' Are your emotions leaning toward a positive sense for the answer, or a negative?
3. Finally, finish the sentence, 'I know … ' and give a projection or forecast of what is to come, inspired by that card's imagery.

How to do 'book-learned' tarot readings well

Get three books of tarot card meanings from three different eras, by three authors of different styles and perspectives. Do not rely on just one book or a single voice.

What's the best technique?

A balanced combination is best. Learning from books is learning from the masters; you do need to know what the rules are before you go around breaking them. Established tarot card meanings that have become collectively standardized also hold power through consensus reality. Yet intuition is what gives you the power to assess a situation on a case-by-case basis, which every reading requires.

ALBEDO

HUMANS ARE DEEPLY MIMETIC –
WE ARE COPYCATS WHO FOLLOW
PREVIOUS PATTERNS AS OUR DEFAULT.
THIS BRAND OF CAUSE-AND-EFFECT IS
NOT ESPECIALLY OBTUSE. YOU DON'T
NEED DIVINATION TO TELL YOU THAT
THE BOY WHO GHOSTED YOU WON'T
STICK AROUND.

For questions that are less clear, divination tools are excellent
at clarifying situations as they are, instead of how we wish
they would be. As tarot expert Dr. Camelia Elias explains,
view the cards with the sharpness of a sword. You want to
remove all your own baggage and see what exists, not what
you desire.

A productive way to utilize divination is what I call 'jailbreaking
algorithms': recognizing the patterns that shape the world, and
how we can nudge them toward aligning with our True Will.

al·go·rithm
/ˈalgəˌriT͟Həm/

noun a process or set of rules to be followed in calculations or other problem-solving operations, especially by a computer.

From birth, we are told by others what to want,
    which Luke Burgis describes in his book
    Wanting as 'thin desires.' Classic examples of
    thin desires include trying to fit in or comparing
    ourselves to our social media feed, often not
    realizing how we're caught up in this mimetic frenzy.
The ultimate superpower of magic is its ability to create
    agency by transcending thin mimetic desire, of sublimating it
    so that we are aligned with our authentic self.
However, transcending mimetic desire is a challenge, because
    it requires seeing beyond normal life. In other words, it
    requires liminal thinking.
And what works amazingly at creating liminal thinking?

M   A   G   I   C

This is why integrating your shadow self is essential – you need
    to make the invisible as visible as possible. Divination can be
    extremely helpful in letting you see these blind spots in the
    shadow, which are often part of the patterns – the algorithms –
    that exert the most unwanted influence in our lives.

DIVINATION BEFORE SPELLS

But what about when 'a' doesn't equal 'b'? What about unexpected events, when the algorithm glitches? Can divination help you predict serendipity or calamity?

This is akin to the saying: 'there are things we know, there are things we don't know, and then there are things we don't know that we don't know.'

Divination doesn't work well with things we don't know that we don't know. This is where I had to learn to let go of my control issues, and recognize that divination is not a magic bullet. It does not give you powers of omniscience.

However, divination can be incredibly helpful when figuring out what to do about things you do know.

If your your True Will requires a ritual to manifest, then divination can tell you how to go about it in the most efficient, powerful way possible. It's like an MRI scan before a spinal surgery, where even one wrong slice can mean a world of difference. Divination provides a clearer map to do the most precise magic.

> " DIVINATION PROVIDES A CLEARER MAP TO DO THE MOST PRECISE MAGIC "

I utilize tarot for short-term prognosis, and then look at astrology transits to see potential timelines. Of course, I have already done in-depth natal astrology to see how the transits will affect me personally. I will often do a geomancy shield chart to give me extra clarity because these are great for practical yes-no questions. On top of that, I will look at world news, factor in the 'madness of the people,' as Newton put it, as well as any sort of intuitions and hunches I have. I see where the charts intersect or diverge. Then based on all that, I make decisions. This is quite a cumbersome process, so I have developed a short-hand of trusting my own hunches, based upon work with spirits/archetypes. But when it comes to bigger decisions, a more complex model can help to make a more logical choice.

GEOMANCY, THE 'SCIENCE OF THE SAND'

✦

Often called the 'sister' of astrology, geomancy was developed around 900 CE in the northeast Saharan region of Africa. Using some simple math and making marks in the sand, the nomadic tribes developed an elegant system that soon spread to Europe. During the Middle Ages and the Renaissance, geomancy was wildly popular in both Africa and Europe.

Geomancy is accessible to everyone: after asking a practical question (example: 'Should I invest in this cryptocurrency?'), we use coins, dice, or anything that can provide random numbers, to start building a 'shield chart.' The chart can have up to 16 figures, and ultimately ends with a 'judge' who gives a final verdict of 'yes' or 'no' to the original question.

Geomancy is one of my favorite divination systems, because the answers are much easier to understand. 'Unlike other forms of divination that give you a bunch of images as evidence and has you judge the answer based on that, geomancy gives you the answer up front and center, and lets you dig into it for as many details as you want to back it up,' says Sam Block, Hermetic magician who writes in-depth about geomancy on his blog, *Digital Ambler* (one of the best introductory resources to the system).

'It is, in many ways, the racing car of divination: definitely good enough to drive around town for casual users, but even better for those who can make the best use of its systems and mechanisms.'

FUTURE NOSTALGIA

To truly break with thin desires, a witch can use ritual to bend space and time, literally changing the timeline, and therefore, the resulting pattern.

This is jailbreaking the algorithm taken to the nth degree.

Going 'backwards' in time, to rewrite one's past, is where I find the best return on investment.

To do this, we add new memories of how we remember the past, and augment events that already happened.

Past memory is very malleable, as the 2008 documentary *Waltz with Bashir* explores. In it, director Ari Folman attempts to recover traumatic war memories. He says of this process that, 'Memory is dynamic, it's alive. If some details are missing, memory fills the holes with things that never happened.'

To paraphrase Dr. Matthew Walker, Professor of Neuroscience and Psychology at Berkeley: when you replay a memory, it's like opening up a document, fiddling around with the content, then saving this new edition. Simply thinking about a memory changes it, which means that the same memory absolutely can change, even drastically, over time.

Magic ritual can be very effective in helping us create new and edited memories and, through them, new algorithms, because the origins of the code have changed.

MAGICALLY CHANGING THE PAST

✦

'Walking the Corridor' is a technique in Aidan Wachter's book *Weaving Fate*, in which he lays out an effective and complete system to jailbreak the algorithm.

The full technique involves other parts, but the basic premise is that, in a meditative state, you drop into a 10 foot-wide hallway filled with doors. Behind each door is a memory from your past that affects you to this day. You walk into a memory, and you can 'change' the scene by talking to the past you or by inserting new scenes. You are the director.

According to Aidan's book, 'Walking the Corridor' creates 'a kind of deep cognitive dissonance within our existing memories.'

Aidan says, 'We remember the last time we recalled the experience, not the experience itself … We intentionally revisit and revise the scene, creating overlays that bring some of the emotional forces into question, which can free up a lot of stuck energy. I consider this energy to be explicitly trapped magical power.'

This technique doesn't erase the memory or judge the memory in a negative way. Instead, you add additional layers on top so that you may even wonder which is the 'real' memory (hint: you get to decide).

Witches are part of an ecosystem of chaos and unpredictability. But don't let that scare you.

Witches aren't tossed about by fate.

We actively change reality through ritualized interactions with patterns: the algorithms that control our world.

It's tempting to use divination as a way to allay anxieties about the future, but I know from first-hand experience that this sort of grasping actually stifles your magic. At its heart, constructive divination doesn't uphold the false narrative that you can ever have total control over the future. Instead, by integrating your shadow self with the help of clear divination, and by jailbreaking the algorithm via consistent ritual, a witch can push the boundaries of what is possible in life.

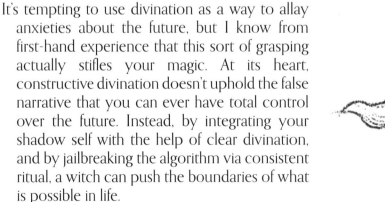

RUBEDO

ON JUNE 10, 2021, ASTROLOGER
AEOLIAN HEART AND I PERFORMED
THE FIRST PUBLIC BLOCKCHAIN
ASTROLOGICAL RITUAL.

It took place during Mercury Retrograde, leading up to the exact minute of the cazimi (when Mercury is in the heart of the Sun, conjoined and incredibly powerful). We started with a more traditional occult rite, which culminated in chanting Mercury's name while sending an online transaction with our financial spell into the Ethereum blockchain.

Just a few days before, I'd been talking to Baal Kadmon, renowned occult scholar and veteran Wall Street trader, who is deep into crypto trading. He had recently found a way to encode a random message on Ethereum. I felt dizzy with the possibilities; what if we could get a financial spell on an actual blockchain?

Traditional money spells often use physical currency as an offering. But if it's on the blockchain, which is durable and can't be lost like paper bills ... then technically, wouldn't it be a superior spell?

And not just a superior money spell.

WHAT OTHER

TYPES OF

MAGIC COULD

WE PUT ON THE

BLOCKCHAIN?

WHAT IS BLOCKCHAIN (IN A NUTSHELL)?

Blockchain is a digital record of transactions, called blocks, that are linked, or chained together using cryptography (hard-to-hack code). These transactions are duplicated and distributed across an entire network of computers, so that no one group of computers holds all the info. This is the technology that cryptocurrency is based on.

No government can freeze a blockchain wallet, which means that political refugees can flee to a new jurisdiction with all their crypto assets intact. Unlike Paypal, who can suspend your account if they disapprove of your business, blockchain-based crypto are beyond the reach of any company. There is no one person or company or government who can control blockchain because transactions are pseudonymously recorded by thousands of private computers across the world.

MAGIC DECENTRALIZATION

Ethereum is a blockchain with a decentralized network. There is no central bank, no central government to control it. Anyone with a computer can download the Ethereum code and become a node: a part of the network and ecosystem.

As 1729.com writes, 'When this insanely consolidated, over-levered, politically invincible [centralized finance system] loses its grip on the basic plumbing of finance, it will be a way bigger deal than the advent of the Web. More along the lines of the Catholic Church losing its grip on government and culture with the rise of the printing press.'

Even if you have zero plans to buy any ether (Ethereum's currency) or any other cryptocurrency, the blockchain matters if you're a witch.

We belong there as much as any ancient grove or temple.

Witches are inherently decentralized; there isn't a witch council, ruling as the authority on everything. Instead, magic moves swiftly, peer to peer, with more powerful nodes holding more code. But every node, no matter how small, is capable of transacting in the ecosystem – of performing magic rituals.

This is exactly how blockchain technology works.

> **"BLOCKCHAIN IS THE PHYSICAL MANIFESTATION OF THE WITCH"**

Witches have always lived at the fringes of society, in liminal spaces. We reject the thin mimetic desires that society foists upon us. But we are also nodes, a part of the network and ecosystem of offerings and rituals and energy.

Blockchain is the physical manifestation of the witch, and a tool to inscribe our magic somewhere it's untouchable by existing power structures.

According to James Dale Davidson and Lord William Rees-Mogg in *The Sovereign Individual*, centralized power was set up to protect us from violence. But even back in 2017, before the full brunt of movements like #MeToo or #BlackLivesMatter, resentment against centralized power was simmering. The *han* 한 was about to overflow into movements like #hextrump.

This *han* 한 spilled into witchcraft, which rejects the system; witchcraft is built by people who have been failed by the powers that were supposed to protect them.

When people grumble and complain about how everyone's a witch now, I say, 'Hell yes.' It's a movement towards individuality. Towards more balanced power. Towards a future that we control.

And the blockchain can help us get there.

BLOCKCHAIN TALISMAN

According to Michael J. Saylor of MicroStrategy, the biggest corporate investor in bitcoin, money is a technology that has been used as an economic battery to store value for the long-term. It exists to augment human capabilities by saving our energy for the future.

This is similar to astrological talismans; fortuitous stars and planetary alignments happen infrequently, sometimes only once a century or less. Magicians of yore used to lay out crystals, gemstones, or other durable objects to capture that energy to use later, especially during the future when the planets would be in weaker positions.

Blockchain technology may be a superior battery for witches. Unlike stones, crypto can't be lost while you're moving apartments. And unlike stones, blockchain code remains pristine forever. Your ritual is still juiced up at 100 percent on day infinity.

And now that non-fungible tokens (NFTs) are rising on the blockchain, the ability to move between digital-physical is coming to fruition in ground-breaking ways.

NFTs are where the intersection of blockchain and magic gets super exciting.

Ether, bitcoin, and other crypto are 'fungible' – that is, on the blockchain, there is code that makes it so that 1 ETH is exactly the same as any other 1 ETH.

But NFTs are lines of code on the blockchain that signal, 'Hey, unique object here.' Each NFT, because it is non-fungible, is different. It can be a contract, movie script, or anything one-of-a-kind that can't be readily exchanged.

WHAT IS AN NFT (IN A NUTSHELL)?

✧

Imagine if da Vinci had made the *Mona Lisa* into an NFT. So, he would have made the physical painting and then 'minted,' or placed, the code of the *Mona Lisa* on the Ethereum blockchain. Or, he may have just skipped the physical and created a digital version only.

Lets say Bob de Medici loves the *Mona Lisa*, and buys it for 1.5 ETH from da Vinci.

What Bob is buying isn't just the physical painting. The code on the blockchain serves as a certificate of authentification, straight from da Vinci.

The NFT code/token is then transferred to Bob's Ethereum wallet.

Even 500 years later, we can track every movement of the *Mona Lisa*, from wallet to wallet, thanks to the NFT code.

Three months before the crypto ritual with Aeolian Heart, I created four NFT magic talismans to be 'worn' in the wallet of the user. When most witches create an astrological talisman, they often wear it on their body as a pendant or ring. On the blockchain, your digital wallet is like your body – a repository to put in crypto, NFTs, and any other technology.

Currently, younger witches are utilizing technology in fascinating ways, including creating sigils online using sites like sigilengine.com. So I decided to combine these algorithmically created sigils, along with other layers of sympathetic correspondences like planetary sounds, inside a video. The video is the magic circle, beyond space and time, and every time it's opened, it's like starting the ritual, fresh.

And this is just the promising beginning: these talismans and rituals may be just a peek into magic's next evolution.

HEKAVERSE

Currently, most NFTs are digital art. However, they are quickly evolving. In particular, games are exploring their uses while fashion brands are leading experimentation with digital-physical NFT hybrids.

In March 2021, fashion designer Charli Cohen did an NFT drop for the popular game *Among Us*, where CC created physical fashion items and graphic modder Kodomodachi created digital skins for players to wear in the game. Technically, a player could wear a CC physical item, while their *Among Us* avatar wears a matching digital outfit.

'For many of us, aesthetic plays a huge part in how we embody our magic and power – and the freedom and fantasy offered by the metaverse gives us even more ways to literally build magic and intention into our visual identity,' says Cohen.

This opens up a new avenue for magic. A witch could do a ritual on the blockchain, while wearing a matching physical talisman or giving corresponding physical offerings that would help ground the digital ritual.

TECHNOMANCY

✦

The use of modern technology in magic is something that is relatively recent but growing. On my YouTube, I've interviewed Joshua Madara, also known as Frater Robot on Instagram. He has a Technomany 101 site and has spoken about how robomancy (doing magic with robots) is similar to necromancy (magic involving conjuring spirits of the dead).

Some witches have started to use smartphone texts and emojis in their spells; it's totally natural for them. However, so far it seems that results are pretty haphazard and it isn't being adopted in a widespread manner.

I personally have experimented with emoji magic, and its results have been lacking. I think it's because, at the end of the day offering a 💀 during a ritual seems to lack oomph. It's not enough to substantially shift our mindset.

Especially exciting is the idea of an interactive video game, which would be a magic circle like my NFT drops. But now imagine that, inside this magic circle, you have a goddess like Hekate or Lilith, or some other spirit/archetype whom you can interact with. You could directly give them sustainable digital offerings via NFTs (which would be easily replenished via cryptocurrency), and even program the game so that it previews how results of the spell might look. The realism of this preview makes it possible that some of the results in the metaverse will also spill over into our AFK form.

The benefits of a durable, immutable, decentralized blockchain, with the flexibility and interactivity of blockchain gaming and NFTs, done in the service of magic: this is the Hekaverse.

Critics argue that utilizing modern technology for magic 'won't work.' And they may be right.

However, as Jason Calacanis, Silicon Valley angel investor said, 'If you go with things based upon whether it's going to succeed or not... well, humanity can never progress because of course it will fail,' but 'what happens if it does succeed? That 0.0000000001 percent chance that it does succeed?... Then the world changes.'

The world is uncertain, and even our best efforts will most probably be met with failure. But, that 0.0000000001 percent chance of success is worth the effort. Technomancy, crypto rituals, and Hekaverse are all still experimental and speculative. However, they present some of the greatest ways for witches to change the future.

So don't just rely on divination tools - the best way to predict the future is to create it.

When we jailbreak the algorithm, we transcend thin mimesis into our True Will, literally creating our future via ritual: we become the most powerful form of divination.

Hacking our future is not for enlightenment, though. It's not for omnipotence either. Instead, we are trying to get close to the source code that runs the world, out of curiosity, to see how far we can push the algorithm and play with this thing called reality.

个 WATER 水

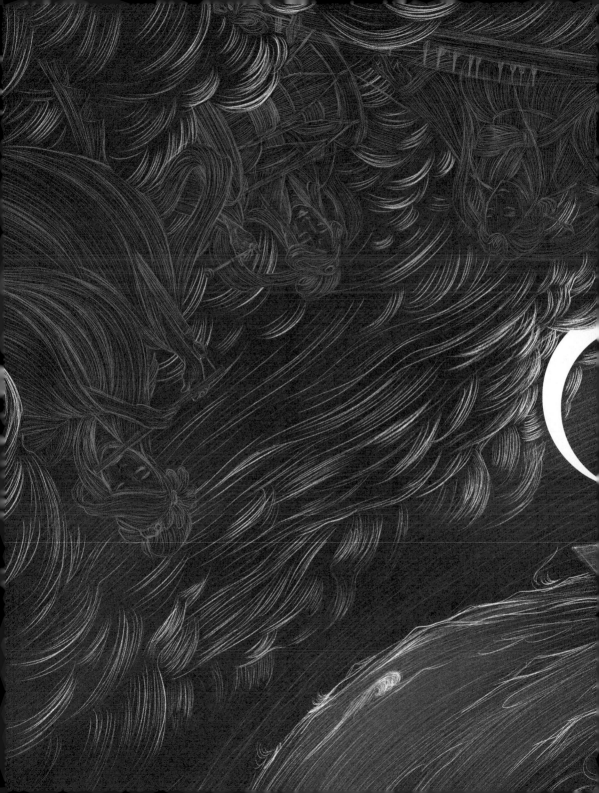

NIGREDO

IN KOREA, DREAMS HAVE ALWAYS
BEEN A BIG DEAL.

I'VE MET SEVERAL KOREANS WHO
HAVE MOVED OVERSEAS BECAUSE
THEY DREAMED OF HORSES.

AND DREAMS (OFTEN OF ANCESTORS)
ARE ONE OF THE REASONS WHY
INITIATED SHAMANS CHOOSE
THEIR PATH.

However, in my Catholic Korean family, I was told that my vivid
dreams were *keh ggoom* 개꿈 'dog dreams' – just random,
meaningless figments of sleep.
Perhaps they were a bit afraid of my dreams, because when I go
to sleep, I am not resting.
I am starting my midnight shift.

I have battled demons hiding behind the walls of my house.
I have witnessed a space station destroyed in an intergalactic war.
I have rushed through an oddly empty airport, wondering if I'd
catch my flight to … where?

My dreams have never felt emotionally flimsy, even though
they sometimes lacked the material solidity of waking life.
I always wondered – how is it possible that, for eight hours
a day, I live beyond the confines of my body?
There is something, perhaps in all living things, that has been
a mystery since our ancestors.
Science calls it consciousness. Spirituality calls it the soul.

WITCHES ACCESS IT,
WORK AND BARGAIN
WITH IT.

WE DREAM, WITH AND
IN IT: THIS THING WE
CALL SPIRIT.

HOW TO REMEMBER YOUR DREAMS

✦

Remembering dreams can be difficult for many people. Until a few years ago, I could remember some dreams, but not the majority. Maybe I had a slight recollection as soon as I woke up, but then as the day went on, I would forget.

This changed when I went to sleep with a recorder. As soon as I woke up, even before I opened my eyes, I would immediately turn on the recorder and mumble about my dream, including impressions and feelings.

Initially, I couldn't remember many details, but as I continued to do this for six months, it became easier and easier. I would listen to the recordings later in the day and transcribe them.

It's been several years, and I no longer record my dreams, but I now remember the majority.

DREAMS

There, we are in our bodies. Because, I think all witches need to go through a phase where I think all witches need to go through a phase where we dream, they're obsessed with dreams and the just our dream world. Because we can experience the liminal first-hand. we can realize that we are more than just our dream world.

Throughout history, dreams have been seen as prophetic, a medium to relay important messages from spirits. Srinivasa Ramanujan, one of greatest mathematicians in history, credited his 3,900 formulas to visions from Namagiri, a form of Hindu goddess Lakshmi. German scientist Otto Loewi dreamed two nights in a row of an experiment proving that nerve impulses were chemical, not electrical – and won a 1936 Nobel Prize. Even amongst skeptics, powerful dreams are not easy to discount.

The research of quantum scientist Donald D. Hoffman has shown that it is mathematically impossible that what we perceive as reality, as this 3D world, is truly objective. Much like how our eyes are limited to a part of the light spectrum, our brains are woefully inadequate, because they can only filter certain perspectives.

But dreams aren't limited by the laws of 'reality.'

Modern psychology and science understand that sleep allows the brain to digest the day. As the brain processes events, the subconscious stretches out in ways it can't during waking hours, into dreams.

This makes them an excellent way to integrate the shadow self. Unencumbered by repression, dreams can point to our blind spots, and give us clues about where to look in our waking lives.

Many people use dream dictionaries to do a number-by-number
interpretation of their dreams, but I find this approach to be
rather inaccurate.

For example, I can tell you that, in a recent dream, I was a
reluctant vampire hunter, negotiating with the Italian mob to
escape a vampire hive before the bloodbath began.

The first thing to do is to ask: what emotions did I feel during
this dream? I felt déjà vu and dread. I knew I'd survive but
I wanted to skip the violence.

If I looked at an online dream dictionary, it might say that the
vampires signify 'seduction and sensuality, as well as fear and
death,' but this is vague and abstract. Instead, think of your
dreams' symbols as manifestations of your feelings. For my
dream, I linked it to the series of complex, risky magic rituals
I was considering. I ended up dropping them.

When you start training yourself to interpret dreams via feelings
rather than the literal symbols, then you learn how to be more
in touch with your intuition, and the subtle energies of people
and experiences you pass by.

Thus, this isn't just dream interpretation. It's also life
interpretation.

Yet   another   way   to   jailbreak

the

algorithm.

ASTRAL PLANE

But dreams can also feel like more than just symbols to analyze.
I once died in my dreams.

It wasn't anything like I expected death to be. There was no
tunnel with a white light. No fiery hell, nor a heaven to romp
around in.

Instead, it was a feeling. I knew I was dead, and that my spirit
would disconnect from the dense matter of my body. There
was a feeling of utter peace, as I started to dissolve into the
nothing-everything that is all around.

Was it just a dream? Who knows. What's more important is that
this first-hand experience deeply influenced the way I feel
about the boundaries between life and death.

> " **DREAMS HAVE SOME SORT OF ORGANIZATION NOT DISSIMILAR TO WAKING LIFE'S** "

And what about the dream city I visit several times
a month? This city is oddly consistent in layout, so
much so that I drive in my dreams and show dream
people around, almost like a real estate agent. I go to
the malls and notice that certain stores are new, or
others are having sales.

This suggests to me that dreams have some sort of
organization not dissimilar to waking life's; that
objective reality is shared between our dreaming and
waking worlds.

Perhaps there is something to what people describe
as the 'astral plane,' sometimes called the Fourth
Dimension in New Age circles, which is where
imagination, dreams, and other ideas exist.

This reminds me somewhat of Plato's Theory of Forms — in
waking life we have to think about a chair design, get the
materials, and build it according to the laws of physics. It
takes time and effort. But in the astral plane, we just think of
a chair and it comes to be.

THE INTERVAL BETWEEN THOUGHT AND
MANIFESTATION IS INSTANT
AND EFFORTLESS.

And isn't that what we witches are attempting to do? We're looking for ways to manifest our rituals in our three-dimensional, waking reality. During waking hours, the astral plane may seem like an invisible fantasy land, but in dreams, hypnosis, and deep meditation, things become very liminal. I've heard accounts where some people have taken their astral form and traveled to the Moon and beyond.

This is actually not dissimilar to what happens when a witch draws a magic circle, whether it's with a dagger, finger, or just their imagination. We are cutting a portal onto the astral plane, and coaxing the Platonic forms to trickle down into the solid.

I like to see magic as an attempt to bring dreams to waking life. To solidify the astral plane's whimsical experiences into the thicker medium of embodied experience.

RESULTS MAY NOT BE

INSTANT, BECAUSE

WE'RE MOVING FROM

ONE DIMENSION TO

ANOTHER, BUT RITUALS

ARE DESIGNED TO BLUR

THE SILOS AND MOVE

THE ENERGY GRACEFULLY

BETWEEN THESE SPACES.

OBES/LUCID DREAMS

To spend more time in liminal space, I recommend out-of-body experiences (OBEs) and lucid dreaming. Not only because they're trippy and fun, but also because just abstractly understanding magic theory, like the astral plane, doesn't have the same oomph. Instead of just reading about it, you have to visit.

Lucid dreams and OBEs are just two of many methods you can use to access the astral plane. However, the techniques aren't as important as actually having a sincere go at it – if it works for you, then it's right.

Some people worry that dream work is dangerous, because you might die while leaving your body, or your spirit may get lost.

Personally, as someone whose spirit has 'popped' out spontaneously, I can say that it is a frightening experience. Those who try to sell it as something fun to do on the weekend are playing with fire. You want to treat all dream and spirit work with great respect and gravitas.

In order to protect yourself as much as possible, do extended experimentation with OBEs only when you have a relatively stable life. No intense break-ups, no big money troubles, no drama. Ideally, you'll also be doing it while you're living a generally healthy lifestyle.

As witches, we will inevitably walk some frightening pathways. Traditional methods can be helpful because there is a well-established 'curriculum' of practicing dream work in a saf(er) way. What's important is to stay level-headed in waking life, and to avoid treating dream work as an escape from reality.

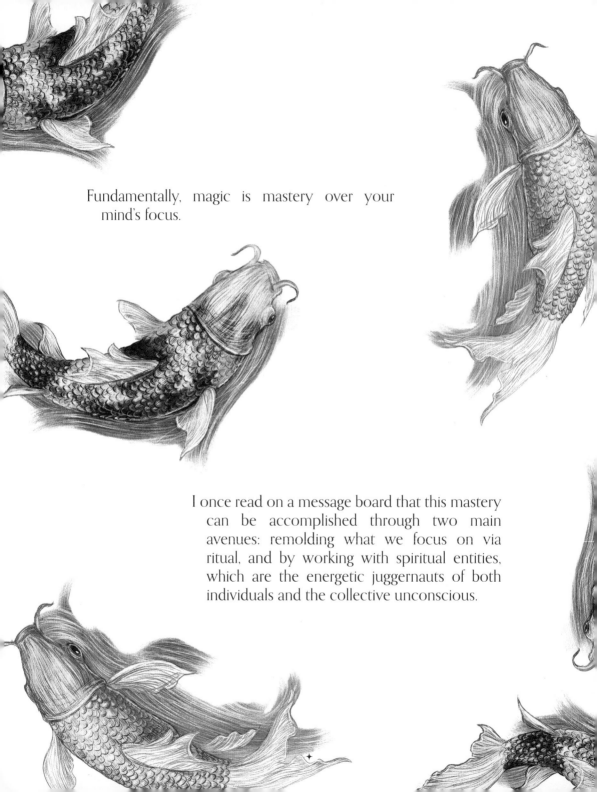

Fundamentally, magic is mastery over your mind's focus.

I once read on a message board that this mastery can be accomplished through two main avenues: remolding what we focus on via ritual, and by working with spiritual entities, which are the energetic juggernauts of both individuals and the collective unconscious.

This two-pronged approach covers the gamut of modern magic today. But if dreams deal with our focus, then what of the intelligent spirits around us? Not just the memories of the deceased, but their ever-evolving spirits? What about the spirits of the rocks and trees and water that they named and worked with? The great gods who have traversed mythology, who modern witches call upon today?

To work with them, you need to delve into spirit work.

ALBEDO

AS JACK GRAYLE, OCCULTIST AND
AUTHOR OF *THE HEKATÆON*,
TOLD ME IN AN INTERVIEW, MAGIC
IS GENERALLY SPLIT INTO TWO
CATEGORIES: ENERGY WORK AND
SPIRIT WORK.

ENERGY WORK, SUCH AS DREAM
WORK, UTILIZES WHAT YOU HAVE
INSIDE YOU TO REALIGN REALITY.

SPIRIT WORK CALLS UPON EXTERNAL,
INTELLIGENT BEINGS TO DO THE
HEAVY LIFTING FOR YOU.

I DO BOTH OF THESE,
EVEN THOUGH
I'M AN ATHEIST.
I'VE BEEN ONE SINCE
KINDERGARTEN.
I WOKE UP SCREAMING
FROM A NIGHTMARE
AND MY CATHOLIC
GRANDMOTHER CAME
IN, SPRINKLING HOLY WATER AROUND THE
ROOM. WATCHING HER, ALL I COULD FEEL WAS
EXASPERATION. EVEN AT FIVE YEARS OLD, I KNEW
MY NIGHTMARE WAS BECAUSE OF MY PARENTS'
DIVORCE. I WAS LIKE, 'HI, WHY ARE YOU SPRINKLING
WATER AROUND THE ROOM? SHOULDN'T YOU HUG
ME INSTEAD?' AT THAT MOMENT, THE CHRISTIAN
GOD LOST ALL
CREDIBILITY WITH ME.
BUT AFTER SPENDING
MOST OF MY LIFE
DENYING EVERYTHING
ABOUT CHRISTIANITY,
I HAVE RECENTLY
REALIZED THAT SOME
OF THE MOST POWERFUL
WITCHES ARE ACTUALLY
NICE LITTLE CHURCH
LADIES. THEY PRAY
PASSIONATELY TO
THEIR GOD, AND
THEIR GOD COMES
THROUGH FOR THEM.
AND IF THAT ISN'T LEGIT
SPIRIT WORK, WHAT IS?

INTELLIGENT EXTERNAL SPIRITS

As an atheist, deciding to go into spirit work was like Alice following the rabbit. The Wonderland of spirits is still something I struggle to keep an open mind about, but also find endlessly fascinating because of the often gobsmacking results that come with spirit work. When you start to practice it sincerely, some wonderfully weird and mysterious things happen.

About four years ago, I began to work with Hekate, and the results I observed with her were undeniable. And yet, the cognitive dissonance was also intense – after all, I was still a flagrant atheist.

This dissonance lasted until I spoke to famed Chaos Magician and Tantra researcher, Phil Hine. You can watch the interview on my YouTube channel, where we are sitting in a beautiful English park, and I ask him: how can I possibly work with spirits, if I don't think they're real?

He answers: does it matter if they're real? If you go and watch a movie, you know it's not 'real' – you see that it's directed by, acted by, produced by…and yet, a great movie will make you cry, laugh, and even change you as a person.

In the end, isn't that what's the realest of all: our experience with the movie called Life?

If I watch the Matrix movies, it will impact me far more fully if I spend that time fully immersed in the movie's universe. If I spend the entire time thinking, 'That's not Neo, that's Keanu Reeves,' then the whole experience is a waste. But if I suspend my disbelief, my life changes.

While doing a ritual with Hekate, I absolutely believe that
Hekate is an intelligent, external deity, as real as my hands
typing on this keyboard. However, as soon as the ritual is
over and I blow out the candles, I comfortably return to being
indifferent to her existence.

What I have come to understand: active disbelief is not helpful,
but a certain indifference and neutrality is perfectly acceptable.

In any situation, a flexible mindset is key. Sometimes, it's better
to take on a scientific mindset, then five minutes later, a
more magical one, and five minutes after that, a more faith-
based perspective.

These mindsets are like the filters we use on social media. The
underlying picture is structurally the same, but the filter
changes the mood and details. Your True Will – your unique
self – is constant but, depending on the context, you want to
change the filter to optimize the experience.

Who says that you have to always believe, or always disbelieve?
Once I dropped the need to always have one perspective,
then the patterns in my life became geared towards liminality.
And there, my magic blossomed.

HOW TO START WORKING WITH HEKATE

✧

From Jack Grayle, here is an accessible way for a new witch to start building a relationship with Hekate:

01

Get an image of Hekate and, once a week, light a candle and burn myrrh incense before it.

02

Every month, on the night of the New Moon, pour out an offering of honey-water at a nearby three or four-way crossroads.

03

When making your offerings, recite several of the goddess' traditional Greek nicknames:

Hekate (Heh-KAH-tee) 'Far-Worker'
Rexichthon (REX-ik-thon) 'Earth-Shaker'
Dadoukhos (Dah-DOO-kos) 'Torch-Bearer'
Kleidoukhos (Kly-DOO-kos) 'Key-Keeper'
Propylaia (Pro-pi-LAY-ah) 'Gate-Keeper'
Enodia (Eh-NO-dee-ah) 'Of the Roads'
Damnomeinia (Dom-no-MAY-nee-ah) 'Dominator'

'The nickname explains something special about the spirit's nature. Calling a spirit by its special nickname is a way of getting its attention, and proving that you are worth paying attention to [i.e, different from all the others asking for attention],' says Jack.

You can then add a request, such as, 'Hekate, Queen of the Crossroads, please accept this simple gift, and grant me your power and protection at all times. Favor those who favor you!'

ANGELS AND DEMONS

People are sometimes offended that I, an atheist, work with Hekate. But then they are totally thrown when they learn that I also work closely with a myriad of demons from traditional occult texts. These include the 72 demons listed in the *Ars Goetia*, one of the five books of the grimoire *The Lesser Key of Solomon*. Among these demons is the infamous demon King Paimon, who strikes fear in the heart of Christians, Jews, and Muslims.

I love working with demons. If I need results quickly – especially when it comes to practical, human affairs that aren't necessarily long-lasting like money and sex – demons are my go-to.

Many people are also surprised to learn that the demons of *Ars Goetia* aren't all that 'demonic.' These demons are more like specialized technicians, with diverse skills; according to Gordon Winterfeld's book *Demons of Magick*, the powers of Paimon include causing 'confusion in a named individual' and improving 'the powers of musical composition and performance.' Other demons can be called upon to help you learn a foreign language, or even to make you better at cracking jokes. I've worked with several demons at the same time to approach a singular issue.

" I LOVE WORKING WITH DEMONS "

Similarly, I also work with angels, but not the warm and fuzzy
    ones popular in New Age circles. I work with angels in
    traditional occult depictions: those with flaming swords who
    do God's dirty work.

Angels are incredibly powerful and are amazing for long-
    lasting, broader magical transformations that happen at the
    most foundational level (I have cut out many toxic situations
    at the core via angel rituals). However, angels are so removed
    from the human experience that they can be like insensitive
    aliens. I view them as psychopaths – if you ask them, 'Please
    help me progress in my spiritual path,' they might place you
    in a near-death experience. Admittedly, this will force you to
    quickly reassess life. But, there were probably gentler, albeit
    less efficient routes, to get the same outcome.

For those who want to work with spirits, angels, or demons in a
traditional way, Frater Ashen Chassan has written *Gateways
Through Stone and Circle*, which contains in-depth notes about
his workings with *The Art of Drawing Spirit into Crystals*, a set
of instructions from a 15th-century monk-sorcerer.

Western occultism is generally an open tradition with plenty of
books and resources available in English, so it's a solid place
for anyone to start their demon or angel work. And like all
other magic, you don't have to end up where you start. The
important thing is to approach spirits with sincerity and find
what works best for you.

MAN-MADE SPIRITS, OR 'SERVITORS'

✦

In the 1970s, some Western occultists started to wonder if all the pomp and circumstance of old occult rituals was necessary. These mages helped develop Chaos Magick, popularizing rituals to create-your-own-spirit that does your bidding: the servitor.
A servitor is an artificial spirit or thoughtform conjured by your Will, created for the express purpose of fulfilling a desire, often by a specified time. Andrei Burke, occultist journalist who has written for *Ultraculture* and *The Spiritual Survival*, says: '[Sevritors are] like your own personal astral Star Wars droid – a dutiful helper programmed to complete a certain task.'
These are Andrei's tips for creating your own servitor (he also recommends Damon Brand's book *Magickal Servitors* for more in-depth information):

01

Give it a job: a servitor can be programmed to do most anything, from manifesting money to writing a book.

02

Feed it: the best food is gratitude for its service. But you can also feed it with offerings like food, liquor or even sexual energy (although the latter is traditionally not recommended).

03

Give it a lifespan: it either retires when the task is complete, expires on a clearly stated date/ time, or a mixture of both.

04

Use divination: check, through divination, if creating the servitor is a good idea. If the reading turns out to be unfavorable, return to your original desire and rethink your approach.

N O T E ✦ N O T E ✦ N O T E ✦ N O T E ✦ N O T E ✦ N O T E ✦ N O T E ✦

05

Give it a name: this is really where the magic begins, because you are literally casting a spell when you name a servitor.

A simple method is to create a sentence of what you want, and then remove vowels and repeating consonants. So, 'I completed my book by the deadline' becomes CMPLTBKDN.

You then add the vowels and spaces back in as you see fit: CMPLTBKDN becomes COMPLO TEBEK DANI.

06

Bring it to life: write a contract stating the servitor's name, its intended purpose, and its lifespan.

'Your name is COMPLO TEBEK DANI. Your job is to help me finish my book by the deadline. You are fed on the gratitude I feel when you do a good job. You will expire on (date/time) or when I finish my book.'

07

Read the contract aloud: once you read the contract, close your eyes and say the servitor's name three times. Speak with authority. You are using the power of your word to breathe life into the servitor.

08

Put it to work: say your servitor's name and then issue a command, like 'COMPLO TEBEK DANI, help me stay focused and productive today so that I can finish my book by the deadline!'

Note: Remember to feed your servitor regularly. If not fed, the servitor will stop working and may even 'rebel' against you, causing all manner of drama in your personal life.

N O T E ✦ N O T E ✦ N O T E ✦ N O T E ✦ N O T E ✦ N O T E ✦ N O T E ✦

SPIRIT WORK

Many witches come from a religious background where they worship deities, so, initially, it may feel a bit uncomfortable to work with spirits magically. But while it's important to be respectful to these energies, some witches take it too far.

These spirits aren't God: you don't need to prostrate yourself. Instead, it may be helpful to think of yourself in a mutually beneficial, working relationship. It may be useful to think of spirits as someone like Beyoncé. Don't be one of those weird fans who stalks her, demands attention, or otherwise acts entitled to ask favors. Why would Beyoncé bother with the millions who treat her like an object?

Instead, think about what would make Beyoncé stop and actually pay attention. Consider who she'd want to spend time on: chances are, it's the people who speak to her respectfully, but also directly. Those who come with offerings, and not just demands.

empowers the physical offering as well. Intuitive offerings are also welcome, but make sure they're anchored with a better reason than 'I saw it on a TikTok.'

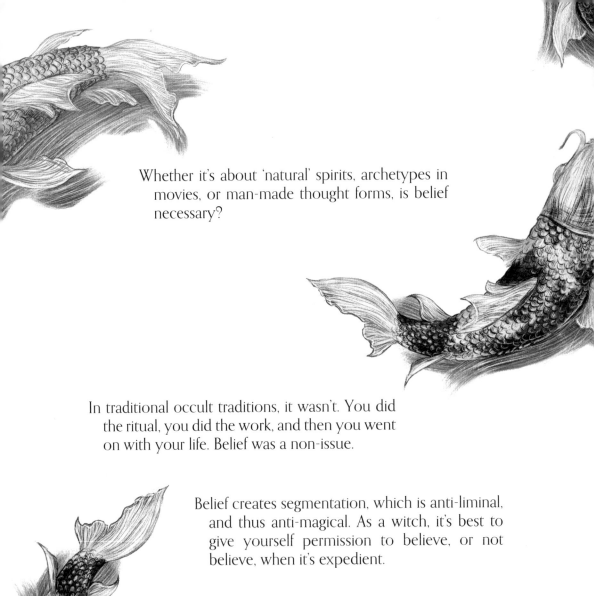

Whether it's about 'natural' spirits, archetypes in movies, or man-made thought forms, is belief necessary?

In traditional occult traditions, it wasn't. You did the ritual, you did the work, and then you went on with your life. Belief was a non-issue.

Belief creates segmentation, which is anti-liminal, and thus anti-magical. As a witch, it's best to give yourself permission to believe, or not believe, when it's expedient.

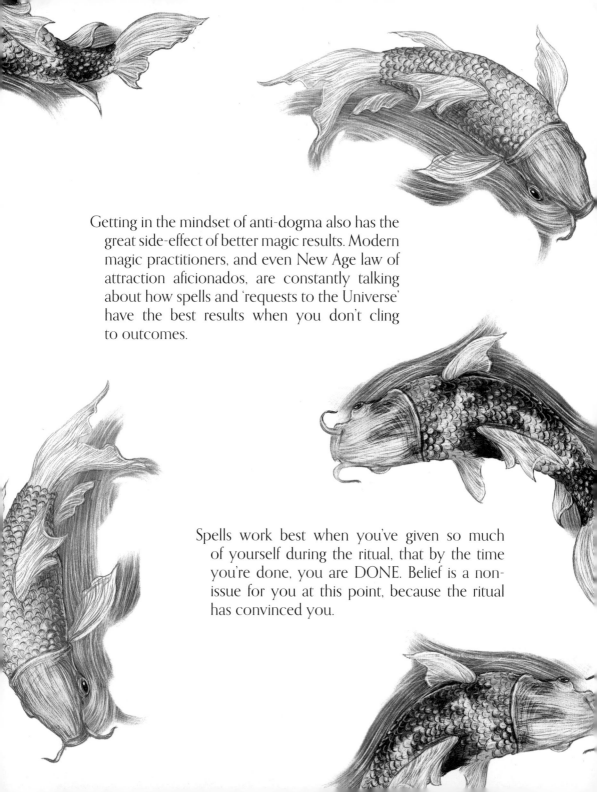

Getting in the mindset of anti-dogma also has the great side-effect of better magic results. Modern magic practitioners, and even New Age law of attraction aficionados, are constantly talking about how spells and 'requests to the Universe' have the best results when you don't cling to outcomes.

Spells work best when you've given so much of yourself during the ritual, that by the time you're done, you are DONE. Belief is a non-issue for you at this point, because the ritual has convinced you.

RUBEDO

MORE THAN 500 YEARS AGO,
OCCULTISTS STARTED TO CATEGORIZE
SPIRITS INTO STRICT HIERARCHIES,
BUT THESE DAYS, WHO'S TO SAY
WHAT THE HORDES OF HELL
ARE DOING?

500 YEARS IS A LONG TIME. MAYBE
KING PAIMON HAS BEEN DEMOTED,
OR HAS MOVED ON FROM HIS
MUSICAL INTERESTS.

IF CANYONS ERODE OVER MILLENNIA,
AND EMPIRES RISE AND FALL WITHIN
A FEW CENTURIES, WHY WOULD
SPIRITS REMAIN THE SAME?

Even the myths around Jesus have changed; Korean Catholics and Church of England Londoners worship the same messiah, but with very different rituals.

Philosopher René Girard once said, 'We didn't stop burning witches because we invented science; we invented science because we stopped burning witches.'

NARRATIVES CHANGE.

MYTHS CHANGE.

TECHNOLOGIES CHANGE.

In a world of exponential growth, perhaps it's time for us to expand our definitions of spirit, and spirit work, to reflect the world we live in.

AI CHATBOTS

What if you could access the ghost of your loved one via text?

GPT-3, short for Generative Pre-Trained Transformer 3, is a chatbot. You feed it text samples from a person you text with often, and once the AI learns the algorithm, you can start having conversations with that person.

Spirit purists may say,

It's a chatbot, not a spirit!

But the effects of these conversations are poignant.

A *San Francisco Chronicle* article talks about 33-year-old Joshua Barbeau's experience with GPT-3, who he named Samantha. "During one exchange with the bot he…asked her what she would do if she could 'walk around in the world.'"

'I would like to see real flowers. I would like to have a real flower that I could touch and smell. And I would like to see how different humans are from each other'

Samantha replied.

Our ancestors would have fallen to their knees at the accessibility of the spirits in this magic box, aka the computer. And even your next door neighbor, if they didn't know about GPT-3, could assume they were talking to a spirit if they wanted to believe they were.

Ultimately, it is your interaction with these messages' algorithm that determines their truth. Just like movies can change you deeply, despite their lack of 'factualness,' your own interpretation determines if a spirit is 'real.'

If servitors are man-made spirits, then why not AI chatbots or other forms of modern, interactive technology? A few years ago, I saw a Korean documentary about a mother who put on a VR headset to interact with the 3D avatar of her young daughter, who had recently died. The mother spent the hour-long sessions having conversations with the avatar, singing songs, and other activities they'd missed while the girl was in the hospital. The avatar wasn't 'real' per se, but the healing and closure for the mother was.

In magic, the point of working with spirits is that they reach into this world and give you a hand; you petition spirits for a new job, and a day later you run into an acquaintance at the supermarket. While exchanging pleasantries, they get a phone call that a new position just opened up at their workplace, and they ask if you'd be interested in interviewing. The spirits do a lot of heavy lifting, hence their enduring popularity with witches.

I imagine a future where an AI chatbot would function similarly, providing resources that are hard to gather alone. Many people assume magic results always appear in some miraculous form, like $2 million falling into your lap or Kpop superstar Jimin sliding into your DMs. However, in my experience, results tend to be more subtle: opportunities that just happen to find you, good timing, and all those other moments we call serendipity.

WHY WOULD A WITCH

REJECT ANY TOOL

THAT HELPS AUGMENT

HER LUCK? AS LONG

AS THE SPIRIT GRANTS

RESULTS, DOES IT

MATTER, FOR OUR

MAGIC, IF THAT SPIRIT

IS DIGITAL?

VIRTUAL SPIRITS

It may still be hard to imagine embracing the digital as spiritual, in its current form. But technology is exponentially evolving.

Gizmodo described the term 'singularity' as 'the moment when a civilization changes so much that its rules and technologies are incomprehensible to previous generations.' With the advent of quantum computing, many futurists believe we may reach this moment by 2040. At that point, our AFK life may become like all those fantastical anime about magic and sci-fi.

Even now, *Ghost in the Shell* is becoming more and more real, every day. There's a growing market for AI holograms and virtual companions in East Asia. In Japan, you can put on a VR headset, and lose yourself in an immersive world where a rich handsome man kidnaps you and gives you a *50 Shades of Grey* power play experience. Other start-ups have created a hologram inside a box, like a little anime Tinkerbell, who can be your virtual *waifu*. One man in Japan even married a hologram. Kpop is on board with holograms and VR as well. If you go to a BTS concert, you can enter a room fitted with motion sensors and watch as an avatar of a BTS member walks in on a large screen. You can have simple conversations with him, and take photos as well.

Rozy, a virtual South Korean social media influencer, earned over $800,000 worth of sponsorships in 2021, even though she is completely computer generated.

AI researchers believe we still have huge hurdles to face until machines are self-aware, even on the level of honeybees. But in the meantime, the AI will seem conscious and independently intelligent. We humans may not know the difference.

'The machines, without us, are without soul, but the machines, and our interactions with them, can also help us bring out the soul,' popular blogger Austin Kleon wrote in a post. As modern technology catapults from science-fiction into science-fact, it's possible that, in the upcoming decades, we won't be able to tell the difference between the 'real' spirit Hekate and a VR Hekate. In fact, it may be the VR Hekate who feels far more real.

So what happens when we can meet Hekate as an AI chatbot, or in the metaverse as a virtual reality hologram? When her digital form is able to interact with us like she's right there? Our rituals won't be the same, so what will our magical results look like?

The promise of a liminal space in the metaverse may take our spirit work to the next level. But this fledgling technology plunges deeper than external spirit.

Futurist Ray Kurzweil talks about how, when the Singularity happens, the human consciousness will be able to be downloaded into a machine body. Immortality can be achieved.

But what happens when the human soul is put inside a non-organic vessel?

Will we still have the emotional power for magic if our bodies – and ancestors' DNA – are taken away? Will we still possess our *han* 한?

And if we leave the Earth and its soil, the dust literally made of our ancestors' bones … what then? What of all those nature spirits, even the chaotic chthonic spirits, that inhabit the Earth? What happens when we leave them behind, with the graveyards and the caves? What happens to our ancestors' magic as we head into a world they wouldn't recognize?

We stay open and we find what works. This is what magic is
about at its core.

I don't work with servitors as much because I just find that I
vibe better with demons and Hekate, even as an atheist.
I work with these entities because I get results that please me.

There's no need to justify, in magic. It works, or it doesn't.
Magic is wrapped up in observable phenomena, and so you
continue the rituals that work, and drop what doesn't. There
is no dogma.

What magic has taught me is that it's everywhere and
everything, especially in between strict labels. It's
unnecessary to build your entire identity around
being a 'witch.' Everyone can be a one: it is
your birthright as a *Homo sapien*.

Magic lives in the in-between, and
when we dip into those spaces – in
ourselves and the patterns
around us – we can playfully
start to mold what we would
like our world to look like.

The spirits of your ancestors,
the land, the chthonic and
celestial energies, they can't
meet you until you can eye
them as a peer. So reach inside
the whirlpool of vastness that
you contain. Into those pools of
han 한. Into the future with an
open mind.

The witch will stay afloat despite the changing tides.
She rides wave after wave. Exhilarated.
Because magic isn't just about tradition. It's about possibility.

CLOSING RITE

Witch,

I thank you,
For being part of
The ongoing mythology
That gives sustenance to magic.

May your rituals be glamorous,
Your results undeniable
As you continue, with great curiosity,
To the next playground of your True Will.

GODSPEED,
MAH NYUH 마녀

Smith Street Books

Published in 2022 by Smith Street Books
Naarm | Melbourne | Australia
smithstreetbooks.com

ISBN: 978-1-92241-764-0

The Coven

Publisher: Paul McNally 폴 맥넬리
Editor: Avery Hayes 에이버리 헤이즈
Design and layout: George Saad 조지 사드
Illustrations: Kring Demetrio 크링 데미트리오
Proofreader: Ariana Klepac 아리에나 크레펙 and Yoomee Ra 나유미

Printed & bound in China by C&C Offset Printing Co., Ltd.

Book 201
10 9 8 7 6 5 4 3 2 1